FIGHTING THE LONG SORROW

A Journey to Personhood

RUSSELL KANE

Outskirts Press, Inc.
Denver, Colorado

Fighting the Long Sorrow
A Journey to Personhood
All Rights Reserved.
Copyright © 2011 Russell Kane
v2.0

Cover Photo © 2011 JupiterImages Corporation. All rights reserved - used with permission.

Outskirts Press, Inc.
http://www.outskirtspress.com

ISBN: 978-1-4327-6594-1

Outskirts Press and the "OP" logo are trademarks belonging to Outskirts Press, Inc.

PRINTED IN THE UNITED STATES OF AMERICA

Dedication

First and foremost, to my parents: thank you for all the hard work you guys did for me with my education and everything else. Secondly, thanks to all of the friends I've had who impacted me all these years: my oldest friend Marla Berkowitz, Reed Gershwind, my deaf "sister" Karen Solomon, Mary DiGiovanna; my NCC colleagues who also teach ASL with me: Jill Burgreen, Stefanie Lewis, and Alec Naiman, my NTID roommate Frank Tempesta, Bill Poje who was my inspiration in Florida in June of 2010 to get off my butt and finally get to write. Third, thank you to all of my elementary school teachers: Mrs. Head, Mrs. Whelan, Mrs. Eisen at Lexington; Miss Contino, Mr. Conklin, Mr. Dickinson, and Mr. Mills at Academy Street Elementary. Fourth, a big holler to my favorite JHS and HS teachers: Mrs. Smith, Miss Bownes, Mr. Morgo, Mr. Riegger, Mr. Killard, Mr. Lawler, Mr. Wood. Fifth, a huge debt to my Hofstra advisor, Dr. Karin J. Spencer. Sixth, pat on the back to KISS-FIST college professors at Gallaudet and NTID: Dr. Mobley, Dr. Lytle, Dr. Cindy King, Dr. Mike Kemp, Dr. John Vickery van Cleve, Dr. Robert Panara. A huge thank you to Carol and Joan, my two speech therapists who had patience with me for fifteen years altogether! Lastly, a THANK YOU to all of my Facebook friends who praised me and sent me congratulations on the book. You know who you are!

Chapter One:
Sunday, March 6th, 1988

"**D**eaf people are not ready to function in a hearing world," said Jane Spilman, Gallaudet University's President of the Board of Trustees, to herself. She was rehearsing this line for when she would step outside the revolving doors and face the crowd outside. She was Gallaudet University's President of the Board of Trustees. She stood inside the huge lobby of the opulent Mayflower Hotel in Washington, DC. The floor was spotless, having been recently buffed and waxed, and there was a huge red-orange rug that covered most of the silver floor. This hotel was where the rich and elite stayed when visiting the nation's capital.

She was finished with the week-long meetings of the board, going through the pros and cons of the three finalists for the presidential job at Gallaudet. It had been very contentious, with one strong deaf candidate, Dr. Harvey Corson, being eliminated in the first round. To many board members, Corson had simply been too deaf-centered. That left two remaining finalists: Dr. I. King Jordan, a deaf professor at Gallaudet, and Dr. Elizabeth Zinser, a well-respected hearing administrator.

Three deaf board members and one hearing member had advocated Jordan's selection. They warned the other members of the consequences if Zinser were to be picked. Only two years ago, a hearing provost had been hand-picked and there had been rumbling on campus, so this could be the last straw for these students. On a vote of 10-to-4, the board went ahead and chose Zinser.

Spilman fidgeted in her black cardigan, dark-colored slacks, and yellow shirt. She looked like she belonged on a yacht instead of a hotel with the mob swelled outside. She looked at the interpreter next to her, dressed demurely in a gray business suit. She looked through the double doors at the angry mob that was sitting right outside the entrance of the hotel. There were so many contorted faces staring back at her.

Theodore Fitzgerald had despair and frustration on his face as he was sitting a few hundred feet away. His face was one of the many in the mob -- which was growing by the minute -- gathered in front of the hotel. Teddy, as everyone called him, had never been the type to rise up and voice his opinion so strongly as he did that night.

Teddy marveled at what had happened just an hour earlier when some guy drove onto the Gallaudet campus in his small, beat-up Volkswagen and hurriedly dumped a stack of press announcements right near the Bison and slunk off, driving away speedily before anyone could grab him. He had stood there dumbfounded with everyone else, approximately fifty people, who were expecting the Board of Trustees to show up announcing the next President of Gallaudet University on that day, March 6th, 1988.

It was a breezy Sunday night just like any other night in Washington, DC, except for one thing: there was a heightened expectation in the air about who would be the next president. Three finalists were in the wings: two deaf men and one hearing woman. Both men signed, the woman not. Dr. I. King Jordan had been born hearing and had become deaf at age nineteen from a motorcycle accident. He had been a beloved professor in the psychology department on campus for many years. He was the favorite of the three candidates due to his tenure on campus, his name recognition, and his intelligence.

Dr. Harvey Corson was an outsider and he was not expected to be selected even though he was a very accomplished Deaf person (note from author: the capital "D" in "Deaf" means he is culturally deaf, as opposed to the small "d" for a pathologically deaf person who avoids ASL and uses speech). The third candidate was Elizabeth Zinser, a total unknown in the deaf world, especially on the Gallaudet campus. She had no background in the deaf education field and did not know any sign language at all. He had been really curious who would be picked by the board members this time. For the past 124 years of Gallaudet's existence, there had been no deaf presidents, so excitement had mounted around the two deaf candidates at this selection process.

When the messenger hired by the board drove off, one or two people in the crowd near the Bison picked up the press release. Teddy stood there and watched as facial expressions turned from hope to shock, and then despair as people started shouting, "This is so wrong! I cannot believe it!" One of the most well-known deaf leaders collapsed like a bag of potatoes. Two women, one on each side, dragged him over to a concrete bench. More people flocked to the Bison from Ely Center and the dorms, as word got out about the selection of Dr. Zinser over two very qualified deaf finalists for the coveted president's job.

Suddenly, someone threw a match onto the remaining papers that were still on the floor and people crumpled up the press release copies, throwing them into the fire. Dr. Gary Olsen, whom Teddy had met before at the previous week's rally, stood up next to the Bison and motioned for everyone to gather around him. Teddy watched the crowd as it got bigger and bigger. By now, there were easily over two hundred people standing about Dr. Olsen as he started to sign something to get everyone together.

Teddy could not believe the board had the gall to go ahead and pick Zinser even after the rally that happened the previous Tuesday. He could quote verbatim what was on the flyer advertising the March 1st, 1988 rally that was held on the campus at the football field. It had been a surreal experience that he never expected to have.

It's time! In 1842, a Roman Catholic became president of the University of Notre Dame. In 1875, a woman became president of Wellesley College. In 1886, a Jew became president of Yeshiva University. In 1926, a Black person became president of Howard University. AND in 1988, the Gallaudet University presidency belongs to a DEAF president. To show OUR solidarity behind OUR mandate for a deaf president of OUR university, you are invited to participate in a historic RALLY!

Teddy chuckled at the memory of the first time he had glanced at the flyer. At first, he had dismissed it as a gathering of just a few students who were disgruntled, and thought nothing would come of it. But as the week went on, he noticed people talking about it in the cafeteria and all around campus. He knew that there was a young group of Gallaudet alumni behind this event who had started planning a few months beforehand. There were even buttons that were distributed all over campus that said: "Deaf president NOW" and were free for the taking.

He decided the night before the rally that he would seize the opportunity to show his pride about Gallaudet and discard his "wallflower" persona. At the education department supply room in Fowler Hall, he grabbed two large poster-size sheets and some yarn and strung together a front/back walking billboard. Putting it under his armpit, he took a black permanent marker and ran all the way down the stairs, across campus, and into his dorm room.

What to say on the two poster sheets? Hmm. Something eye-catching…aha, how about "Deaf President NOW 1988!" On the front, that would be good. As for the back, "Go for it – GU, Deaf Prez in "88." Yeah, that was perfect. He went ahead and used his artistic abilities to design the layout, and realized he had one of those bumper stickers. Where should he place it? His forehead! Nobody knew what he was up to and he wanted to surprise everyone with his newly found deaf pride.

The next morning, after breakfast, Teddy donned the billboard and walked down to the football field for the upcoming rally. People parted for him, staring at his new outfit down to the forehead bumper sticker. Many gave him a thumbs-up. He felt really good and smiled, nodding at everyone. Some just stared at him, as they knew he was a very passive person and this was quite the change for him.

Suddenly, a photographer ran over to him. "That is so cool!" he mouthed slowly. "Come on, stand over here at the fence in the front. That is a great place for you!"

Teddy could see people mingling about on the track. There were some people making signs. One said: "Jews, Catholics, Women, Black — NOW IT'S TIME FOR DEAF!" Another: "DEAF PRESIDENT NOW! ZINSER OUT!" He fit right in with these other signs. Students continued to trickle to the bleachers. There had been an estimated 1,000 turnout, but from what he could see, there was more than that now. Good! Let the board see how strong the sentiment was and pick a deaf president. How could they not?

During the rally, the repeated theme was: "The time is now!" The students loved it and kept signing it throughout each speech. He noticed another sign near him: "Are you a racist? Earist?" He loved it, quite clever. There were many speakers at the rally, including nineteen speakers from various states and organizations such as the National Association of the Deaf, World Federation of the Deaf, the College for Continuing Education, and even the Kendall Elementary School student body!

Speeches were made, all on the importance of a deaf president being selected by the board that coming Sunday. He had listened to each speaker talk about the efforts that were made to contact congressmen and senators. Reaction from those representatives and senators had been favorable and many of their offices wrote a letter to the board advocating a deaf president's selection.

One speaker talked about how Senator Bob Dole of Kansas and Senator Robert Graham of Florida were the first ones to respond to the lobbying of the students, alumni, and faculty that previous month. The crowd went into a frenzy at the mention of those two senators and their support of the selection of a deaf president who would be the first in Gallaudet's history. That had been quite a memory for Teddy as his focus returned to the present. He remembered when Paul Singleton had remarked at the end of the rally, inviting everyone to join him on Sunday night to either celebrate or "discuss a course of action." This was it!

"Let's all march over to the Mayflower Hotel! That is where Spilman and the board are staying right now. We must tell them how we feel about this mockery!" exclaimed Dr. Olsen. The crowd's hands waved through the air. Others called for a blockade of Florida Avenue's traffic to call attention to the way the crowd felt at the moment. Teddy could feel the emotion crest inside him, and this was a totally new feeling that he had never felt before. He ran from the Bison to the front entrance of Gallaudet with the crowd of people, and all of a sudden everyone stood right on the edge of the sidewalk along Florida Avenue. He felt like he was right on the precipice of Mount Everest, about to drop over 10,000 feet.

Faces looked at each other, wondering who would be the first to step onto the street. Finally, one man did. Then a second one. Teddy could not feel anything in his body, even as his feet and legs propelled him off the sidewalk onto the street in the face of upcoming cars. To his relief, a fourth person followed, then a fifth. This opening sequence was all the crowd needed. Hordes of people walked onto the street and then someone yelled to sit down, so they all did. Cars screeched to a halt in both directions.

Teddy looked in amazement as hundreds more students came running from the campus onto the street. Everyone was locked arm in arm, solidified in their mission. Uh-oh! Cops came from all directions, sirens flashing. He wondered where Rhonda was. Rhonda! He wished she was with him on this night. What a special girl that was. She was from New York just like he was and they were both from Long Island. Rhonda was hearing and signed fluently. Oh, how he wished Rhonda would say yes to his asking her out, but she had her heart set on someone else at Catholic University. Rhonda was probably in Clerc Hall doing homework for Monday's classes. Luckily, he had finished his readings, knowing the presidential announcement would be foremost on his mind. He just did not know how much that would be true until right now. He looked to his right and his left.

There was Luis! His crazy, wild roommate from Texas. Luis had this maniacal expression on his face and he was right in his element. Teddy could only imagine what was going through Luis's mind at that moment, as he had witnessed Luis's rants in the cafeteria the whole week prior to this at dinner time about the protest and what would happen if Zinser was selected. Everyone had laughed it off, saying there was no way a hearing person would be picked THIS time. Looked like Luis had been the prophet, and everyone was talking to him now.

Cops stood around everyone who was sitting down. They had white portable cuffs on their hands, ready to arrest everyone. Teddy thought about his parents and laughed out loud. He could only imagine the looks on their faces, getting a phone call from a local DC jail. Their goody-two-shoes son, never having broken the law, now behind bars in the slammer. That would really go over well in their local town on Long Island! Teddy's two hearing younger sisters would have a blast with the protest at school, bragging about their older brother who was walking among the jail population of America.

Jack and Elise Fitzgerald were among the elite on Long Island. Jack was a prominent businessman in Little Neck and Elise was a college professor of literature at Queens College. Rosemary and Kathleen were seventeen and thirteen, respectively. There had been a long time in between Teddy's birth and Rosemary's, as Elise had a hard time adjusting to Teddy's deafness, making decisions about where to send him to school. Good thing Uncle Benny had come to the rescue when Teddy was born. At the time, Benny had been a up-and-coming lobbyist who worked with the big-time politicians like JFK, Eisenhower, and Truman. He had a lot of pull in Washington, DC.

So, when Teddy's father needed some favors, he turned to Benny, who then got the entire FItzgerald family moved to Boston, Massachusetts, enabling Teddy to attend the Clarke School for the Deaf with his father stationed at a nearby military office. *Benny would love this too,* mused Teddy. Even though Benny was prim-and-proper when he was working, he did have his wild and fun side that very few people got to see.

As Teddy scanned the crowd, now forming a mob scene, he wondered how Mom and Dad would react. After all, they had been decisive about everything in his life up to now. After his birth and diagnosis of profound deafness in both ears, his mother had quit her teaching job to stay home with him and teach him full-time while his father finished up his MBA.

In fact, it was his paternal grandmother, Betty, who had first suspected his deafness when he was six months old. Even though she had never finished high school, she was a very smart woman who would not let anyone dissuade her when she made up her mind. Grandpa Jack adored Betty and was putty around her, as he would do anything for her. They persuaded Teddy's parents to get him tested for deafness, so that was how he had been diagnosed so young, as the technology in the '60s was not as sophisticated as it was in the self-centered '80s.

When his father finally quit the Air Force, they moved back to New York, where both sets of grandparents lived. Teddy could only imagine what it had been like for his parents living so far away from their folks, as they were very close. He was glad his father had the sense to leave before being drafted into Vietnam. In fact, some higher-up in Washington had called him up and asked him if he wanted to help with the medical effort over there and his dad had yelled point-blank into the phone, "HELL NO!" and hung up, slamming the phone back on its receiver. Good thing too, or his dad might not have been there for his mom when he grew up.

Then, it had been a rough road being mainstreamed in third grade with no deaf friends around him. Luckily, he made a fast friend in Maureen who became his "girlfriend" in third, fourth, fifth, and half of sixth grade before she had to move away due to her family's breakup after her parents divorced. When Maureen moved away, Teddy's social life suffered. With her around, he had been popular among her friends. Any friend of Maureen's was a friend of theirs.

He saw Maureen two years later on the school bus in eighth grade. He had stayed after school for some extra speech lessons and tutoring. Upon seeing her, Teddy had been overjoyed -- then he was devastated when she didn't even talk to him. Teenagers! He remembered it was raining outside and that matched the tears running down his face as he stared through the fogged-up window all the way home. They were so cruel at that age. This was the girl whom he had his first kiss with, the first walk hand-in-hand with, piano lessons, soup lunches on the weekends.

Sixth grade was especially rough. One day, Teddy was among the big kids in his elementary school and the next, he was a pipsqueak sixth grader walking among taller, bigger boys in seventh and eighth grade at the sparkling new junior high school. This was where he first met Jennifer, or Jenny as everyone called her. She had come from the other elementary school class which had seen its sixth grade class infused into Teddy's class as they moved to the new junior high school that spring semester. Jenny was tall, beautiful, and had the most dreamy eyes. He had such a big crush on her until twelfth grade.

Oh, the efforts he had made to win her heart. Once, when she was really sick with mono and missed school for a week, he had ridden his bike to her one-floor modest home on the other side of town. It was a beautiful Saturday afternoon after school had let out on Friday. Feeling good and sure of himself, he dismounted his bike and gulped when he saw someone's legs protruding from a 1980 black Camaro. This guy, whoever he was, wore an old pair of shoes. Could it be her brother?

"Ahem, excuse me!" Teddy half-shouted. Oops, he'd better be careful. Too often, he would talk louder than necessary because he could not hear himself even with the two hearing aids he had which were top of the line, made by Oticon. He had a profound hearing loss of 100 dB in both ears, so he was unable to hear on the telephone. Too often his deafness had led to funny episodes and misunderstandings.

When he was growing up, he used to fight a lot with his sister Rosemary over trivial things. Every time he hit her, his mother would say something to him that appeared to be: "Polish her eyes!" Teddy always thought this was the most ridiculous thing anyone ever said to him. For years, he would ruminate and try to figure out what the heck Mom wanted him to do, exactly. Finally, when he was ten, he found out about the word "apologize" and realized that was what Mom had said all along. He chuckled at the memory. But enough of memory lane. Time to move on with his mission here and now.

The sneakers moved suddenly and the legs slid out from under the car. Uh oh. It was no brother – it was her father! He recognized the dad from another time when he had seen Jenny with him in town a few months ago. The dad's head finally was visible and his facial expression was one of confusion; then his expression softened as he recognized Teddy from Jenny's classes. He knew Teddy was a nice boy who had a crush on his daughter. He thought it was very harmless.

But this boy was Catholic and his daughter was a devout Lutheran so there was nowhere to go for this relationship. He had even made sure his daughter knew that. As a result, for years, she had cried herself to sleep at bedtime because she kept refusing him asking her out. She even had to get a boyfriend at school to put up a pretense to keep Teddy at bay. He had thought his plan was working, and now here was Teddy again. Persistent fellow. He had to give him credit for trying since seventh grade, and now they were in eleventh grade.

He still wanted to be nice to Teddy. It was incredibly brave of this boy to come to their house all by himself. Obviously, he had heard about his daughter's serious illness and wanted to tell her something. Teddy stood there fidgeting and his lips were trembling. This poor young man! He'd better put him out of his misery.

"Teddy, isn't it?" Mr. Donnell hoisted himself up from the ground as he looked at him. He was a big man, 6'4" and muscular. He used to be a boxer. Pugilist was a better word for it, as he had never really made it out of the gym into featured bouts. His face was typical of a boxer. His nose was crooked from all the punches that had landed on his nose. He was like Rocky Balboa and when the movie came out, everyone had teased him about it. This Sly Stallone had "stolen" his idea, as he was thinking of a story about himself.

"Yes, Mr. Donnell, my name is Teddy and I am Jenny's classmate in math and English honors classes." Mr. Donnell didn't realize that Teddy was in not one, but two honors classes. Impressive, especially for a deaf boy. But he was still a Pope lover and that was a no-go for him.

Teddy went on to say, "Is Jenny home now? I would like to give her something in person." His hand slid into his pants front right pocket. "Is it OK if she comes out for a second? Here is a pack of Wrigley's spearmint gum to keep her mouth from becoming too dry. I can wait for her to come out and talk for a second."

Mr. Donnell chuckled to himself. Wasn't this sweet? Too bad the Lutheran boys at church were nothing like Teddy. Chivalry wasn't dead and this proved it. "OK, Teddy. Be right back with her. Wait out here." He opened the front door and went inside, closing the door behind him.

Teddy was very nervous all of a sudden. He felt foolish and wanted to disappear right there and then. Too bad there was no Star Trek transporter where he could dematerialize in just seconds and end up somewhere else! His stomach started to feel like it had butterflies in it. This was not a good idea after all. Oh jeez, Jenny was going to come outside any minute. He better hightail it or have to face her! He quickly mounted his bike and pedaled furiously down the street, halfway to the school they attended.

Out of breath, he stopped the bike, slamming on the brakes. His neck turned and he could see a small figure in a white robe open the door of Jenny's house, and come out on the front porch steps. The face looked around and the figure stood there for a few seconds. Then the person, presumably Jenny, went back inside and closed the door. Whew, that was a close call. Now he wished he had stayed put and talked to her. What a chicken he was with girls!

She did not ever say "yes" to his repeated attempts asking her out. He had even recruited his little sister Katie into calling her one afternoon for a measly buck and she hung up on her in just a few seconds. That had been such a bummer. Then, at high school graduation, he saw Jenny one more time before walking away to face his life without her.

Teddy knew life had its epiphanies, with major decisions that are made in just a few minutes out of months and years in one's life. The first one he could remember making happened one afternoon in the spring of 1981 after he had come back with his parents to visit several colleges in Washington, DC. He had gone to see American University, George Washington University, and Gallaudet University.

He could remember the day they drove to DC to see the two hearing universities and Gallaudet. At American University, the girls had flocked to his dad, who looked good for his age. Funny, when his dad had been in high school, he had been a major nerd with a serious case of zits and geekness. He was always afraid of the girls until he met Betty Cooperman, who was one of the popular girls a year behind him. He had been a sophomore while Betty was a freshman. They took the same subway ride to Friends Academy in Brooklyn and they started going out. They had remained steady throughout college and had gotten married at age twenty-two.

It was funny how American had ended up with the interviewer who called Teddy into his office for the official question and answer session that was required for all prospective students there. Teddy freaked out when the guy blithely commented, "You are such an attractive candidate," when he was so obviously gay, with the preppy clothes he was wearing and his mannerisms. Teddy was so relieved to get out of there and walk away quickly with his parents. George Washington University had been more intimidating with the caliber of students that attended there, even more so than American.

Gallaudet, that was a totally different story! When he walked into the Provost's office and showed her his transcript, her eyes had widened and she motioned for him to wait right there. She disappeared into another office for a few minutes and came back out to say, "Teddy, we are prepared to offer you a half-off scholarship right on the spot. Your grades are really impressive, top ten percent of your class and all these rigorous classes such as geometry, trigonometry, biology, and honors English. Your SAT scores are 1170 with 530 Verbal and 640 Math. We would love to have you here!"

Teddy had been rendered speechless and he came out of the office to tell his parents. They went over to Ely Center and that had been quite a shock, seeing everyone in there eating and what seemed to be an endless wave of flailing arms all over the building. The cafeteria near Carlin Hall had been more of the same. This had scared Teddy out of his wits, as he was not fluent in ASL yet. Looking back on this experience, Teddy regretted not coming to Gallaudet as a freshman to start a new life away from home. But he needed something with a connection to the Deaf world and that would end up being RIT/NTID.

He was scheduled to drive to Pennsylvania to see Muhlenberg College, among other schools. Upon entering the house, he saw his mother in the kitchen making dinner and he sat down at the table. He felt the weight of the world on his shoulders and he looked at his mother. She knew something was wrong and stopped what she was doing.

"Teddy, are you all right? You look like something is on your mind. Spill the beans!" That was his mother, all right. Anytime she wanted the truth out of him, she would tell him to spill the beans. That meant she was serious about having to know everything. There was no going around her once she had her mind set on something that she wanted to find out from anyone.

He looked at her with a forlorn face that showed how he felt: frustrated and helpless. "Mom, I have made a decision. I am not going to a hearing college, not after all those years at a school where I had very few friends and nobody that signs. I have learned sign language the past year and I want to be around deaf people all the time! I want to feel like I am the same as everyone else and not the freak show that I feel like I am right now!" His breathing became labored and he had to remain seated to calm himself. Breathe, Teddy, breathe.

He could remember feeling that way back in 1981. It had been a pivotal moment that led him to attend NTID in Rochester, New York. He got his degree in criminal justice with honors in 1986 and he had been very happy up there. Yet, he wound up at Gallaudet, going for a master's in deaf education that spring semester in 1988, which was why he was at Gallaudet tonight as a special undergraduate student, on March 6th, 1988, in the middle of the biggest event in deaf history ever recorded. Now he was here with 300-400 other students, surrounded by cops, then off they went to the Mayflower Hotel where they were standing and shouting for the board's attention.

Finally, someone came through the hotel front doors. Jane Basset Spilman! In person! Of course, there was an interpreter with her. She couldn't sign a word, yet she was the board president? That had to be the biggest joke of all time! How the heck had she become a leader at Gallaudet, leading the board of trustees at the Deaf Harvard? Rumor had it that it was money that spoke louder than any other qualification to be on the board and, of course, she came from the big furniture company that was in North Carolina, so that seemed to be the status quo at other universities where big-time donors bought their way onto prominent boards for clout and power. It just did not make any sense to him at all.

Teddy watched, bemused, as the interpreter frantically waved her arms for everyone's attention. Spilman seemed to be gathering self-control, her hands squeezing fists so hard that her knuckles became white. She cleared her throat and started to speak. It was this very particular moment that she uttered the most inane sentence in the history of deafness: "Deaf people are not ready to function in a hearing world." Teddy's mind exploded as the interpreter signed that and a rage built up inside him, as this was the straw that broke the camel's back.

All of the memories flooded into Teddy's brain of his upbringing in a hearing non-signing family, public schools where no students signed, there was no PL 94-142, no captioning, nothing in his life that gave him reason to believe he was ever going to feel like he belonged.

All of those nightly dinners where his family had conversations about the day and he was just sitting there like a lump eating his food, then having to wait until everyone was finished before he could leave the table. There was a steadfast rule that was followed about everyone not leaving until the last morsel of food was chewed, but Teddy finally broke that rule as a teenager, as he stormed off to watch TV with the newly captioned news with Peter Jennings. Anything was better than sitting down at the table, not understanding what was happening.

Then there were the family gatherings where Teddy was always bored, having no clue what anyone was talking about. His sisters Rosemary and Kathleen would be laughing at something their grandparents said, or Uncle Benny whose house they went to often, upstate in Carmel. They also went to Grandpa Joe and Grandma Dolly's house in Brooklyn for dinner, where the same situation played out with different players.

It had built up over the years inside Teddy, and finally he had had enough at this very minute as Spilman uttered that infamous phrase that resounded in his soul and stirred awake the deaf pride that he had never acknowledged until that night. Now she was being dismissive of deaf people in general.

Funny, that reminded him of how he felt around his family. Nothing new! But this time he and everyone else in the crowd at the Mayflower

Hotel were doing something about it instead of just sitting back. It was time to roll up their sleeves and fight back at the paternalism that was evident here.

Teddy got up and fought through the crowd, looking for Luis. Upon finding him, their eyes locked and they grasped hands in solidarity. Their relationship had gotten off to a rocky start just two months before in January when the semester started. Teddy remembered the first day of school. Luis had taken over the entire dorm room, thinking he was set for the semester having a room all to himself, but at the last minute, Teddy was assigned to this room in Cogswell with him.

Luis was not happy to be bunking, especially with a graduate student. Teddy had told Luis that he would not be in the room much because he would be studying with graduate students in Clerc Hall, so that quieted Luis down to the point where they could have a civil relationship for the rest of the semester. Now they were just two faces in a crowd, all united under one banner.

"Can you believe this, Luis? Your prediction was right on the money, roomie!" Teddy exclaimed. Luis beamed back at him and laughed. "What do you think will happen tomorrow, Luis? What are the leaders planning?"

"The leaders are now talking about it already -- I bet they will block the gates so the faculty can't enter the campus, and we will get classes cancelled!" Luis smiled, eyes twinkling. "Don't put it past us, we will do it!"

"Luis, are you kidding me? Block gates? How?"

"Don't worry, Teddy, it will happen. Mark my words. I think I know how...hey, here come the leaders. Off I go! By the time you wake up tomorrow, you will see for yourself, Teddy. Don't worry. We are all going to work together. We may have a job for you, so be on the lookout in the cafeteria. OK?"

Luis playfully punched Teddy's right arm and walked away to join the four leaders. Teddy watched Luis march off, looking at his receding figure.

Good old Luis! Boy, was he wrong about his roommate. So young, at twenty, and already a leader among his peers at Gallaudet. A freshman! Teddy was twenty-four and had nowhere near the leadership skills of Luis. That's what you get for attending a mainstream school all those years, Teddy! Proof a residential school for the deaf spurred on leadership skills. Plus that Youth Leadership Camp that he'd heard all about for the past two months.

He wished he had known of that camp. Damn his parents! They probably had known or should have, in their investigation of summer programs for him to attend. He had gone to two sleepaway camps, both disasters. Camp Kent had been the absolute worst, all hearing kids and not a single deaf kid in the bunch. His parents and he had been fooled by the owner's bells-and-whistles slide presentation at the Fitzgerald house on Long Island.

He remembered his dismay when the bus rolled into the camp that July day in 1978. The bunks were almost beyond repair, leaking water, soggy cots. He got into fistfights almost every day because other boys in his bunk were mocking his hearing aids and ineptitude in sports. He refused to shower for the last four weeks and upon returning home he had to be taken to the doctor for special cleaning to prevent infection and germs from spreading.

Camp Lenape the following summer had been just a little better. The boys there were much nicer, but the allergy and asthma attacks every night crippled Teddy, who had to sleep in the infirmary under the watchful eye of the doctor. Finally, after ten days and fifteen pounds lighter, his parents drove up to Lenape and picked him up, having learned their lesson with Kent. On the way home, they stopped at a Friendly's where Teddy ate a sumptuous meal including three hot dogs, a hamburger, and a chocolate hot fudge sundae. His parents sat there shocked as Teddy ate hot dog after hot dog, then the burger, and topping it off with the sundae.

"Hungry, Teddy?" Mom had asked him.

Teddy nodded vigorously. "You have no idea what it was like being in the infirmary ten nights in a row, not being able to breathe and not having anything to do. I didn't even have enough energy to eat anything! I lost fifteen pounds by the time you guys wised up and got me. I did shower every night, though. Didn't want another doctor's visit like last summer. Remember?" The edges of his lips curled up and he blinked back tears.

"You are too funny, Teddy." Dad had chuckled as they all remembered what the doctor had exclaimed last summer about Teddy's absolute state of filth, as if he had come out of the sewer.

YLC would have been really good for him and he would've been a leader at this time, like Luis. Every summer, YLC took sixty-four deaf campers from all over the country and taught them leadership skills that they could use in their lives upon returning home. Many of them became leaders in the deaf community, working as teachers, lawyers, doctors, administrators, and other productive jobs. The stories he had heard were inspirational.

Yes, the four-week camp was notoriously rough, but they did learn invaluable lessons about themselves. They became better citizens, building up self-identity and confidence. It had started in 1970 and hundreds of campers had been given this enriching experience ever since. Too bad he had not gotten to experience that.

Now Luis was at the forefront of the new protest while he was going to be left back in the trenches. Maybe he would learn a thing or two. He was game for it. Back to campus for tomorrow. Another day! Bed never looked so inviting as it did tonight for Teddy. He dragged himself under the covers at 1 a.m. All the emotional stress and physical exertion had taken its toll on him.

Chapter Two:

Monday, March 7th, 1988

Teddy slept soundly until around 9 a.m. He had forgotten to set the alarm. Damn it! Now he was going to get into trouble for missing classes. Teddy's mind was fuzzy. Why was he so tired? Did he party late last night? Slowly, his mind started remembering bits and pieces. The stack of papers, the guy zooming off in his small car. The burning. People crying, running. Blocking traffic. Speeches. Running again. The hotel. Spilman! Oh, the protest! What was going on with that, anyway?

Yawning, he forced himself to wake up and get out of bed. It was time to get the scuttlebutt about what students planned to do today. Funny, everyone picked on Teddy for using the word "scuttlebutt" growing up. For some reason, he liked that word he had seen in a military novel, *Battle Cry* by Leon Uris, and started using it instead of "gossip." He strongly felt that he could have been a soldier, even a Marine, in his past life.

His favorite color was hunter green, with khaki a close second. Every time he saw Camps Lejeune and Parris Island, he felt very familiar with the surroundings as shown in their pictures. *An Officer and a Gentleman* hit a nerve when he watched Louis Gossett, Jr., yell obscenities and hurl insults at the new officer candidates. The same thing had happened with another movie, *Full Metal Jacket* with R. Lee Ermey playing the sadistic drill instructor. It just seemed more apropos for him to use, for whatever reason.

Yawn -- it was going to be a long day full of surprises, that was for sure. Those showers were not the best. Trickling water at best. It was better than nothing. Where was Luis? Of course! Busy outside with the leaders who all came from deaf families. Interesting. That had not occurred to Teddy before. Greg Hlibok, Jerry Covell, Tim Rarus, and Bridgetta Bourne all had strong roots in the deaf community, deaf parents, deaf grandparents, deaf siblings, all YLC alumni, schools for the deaf. Four for four.

Luis was just like them, but no deaf relatives. He had gone to YLC also and attended a residential school, staying in the dorms Monday through Friday, so that sort of counted. Teddy chuckled, wondering what he would have been like if he and his parents had decided to send him to MSSD, Model Secondary School for the Deaf, right on Gallaudet's campus. That would have been a blast for sure. Back then, when he was in high school, he had been too scared to move away from home. Look at his misadventures at sleepaway camp. It would have been a disaster if he had gone to MSSD, but that was his parents' fault, as he had no independent skills, no idea how to cook, or do laundry.

That reminded Teddy of a funny story when he was eleven. It was a good example of how deaf people thought of everything in concrete, literal terms. One early morning he wanted to bake a cake and surprise everyone before they were awake. He came downstairs to the kitchen and found a cake mix. Realizing he did not have enough of all the ingredients, he figured he would halve the size of the cake and halve everything he needed to make it. Shrugging his shoulders, he went ahead and followed the instructions. Only if everyone could see him now, busy bee in the kitchen where he never spent any time except eating! Finally, the cake was ready to be put in the oven.

Teddy marveled as the cake slowly rose and the minutes flew by one at a time. He then took a mitt (which was from Grandma Betty's time, worn as it was) and took the pan out of the oven. Mmm, it smelled so good. Wait until the icing. Teddy was so excited -- he took the sweet icing and lathered it onto the cake. The smell obviously was very strong as his parents and two sisters came down the stairs with puzzled facial expressions. Teddy in the kitchen baking a cake? What was the world coming to these days?

Teddy turned around, stood up proudly. "There is your cake. Let's eat it for breakfast! Who wants to try it first?"

His parents and sisters looked at each other. Katie, being the youngest, said, "Sure! I love cake and I want to try it!"

Teddy looked at her with sad eyes. "Katie! Remember you are diabetic, so let's have Rosemary taste it. Very sweet!"

Rosemary clapped her hands and jumped up and down. "Yeah!" She took a knife out of the drawer next to the dishwasher and then a plate from the cabinet above the sink. Cutting a piece of cake, she put it on her plate and then took a bite. All of a sudden, her face became contorted. She started gagging and suddenly pulled out the trash bin, spitting out the entire bite.

"Hey, what's wrong with my cake, Rosemary? I made it just this morning. Mom and Dad, try it."

They did not look too happy, but they both took a piece of cake and bit into it. Just like Rosemary, they spit out their cake into the trash. Teddy could not believe it. "Impossible! I have to try it myself. Let's see..." Ugh! The cake was horrible, worse than the yellow medicine he had taken when he was younger, for his asthma. This was like poison! Spit it out! What could he have done wrong?

"Teddy! What did you do to make this cake taste so bad?" asked Mom.

"It does not make sense! I halved all of the ingredients and made half-cake. That is logical, so it should taste the same!"

Mom and Dad laughed so hard that their eyes became wet, tears running down their cheeks. "Oh, Teddy!" exclaimed Mom. "You just cannot halve some ingredients and leave others at full-size to bake a cake. It does not work that way. Nice try though. It was good to see you making something." Dad chuckled and put his arm around Teddy.

"Son, let the women bake the cakes, and we can do the grilling, OK?" His eyes twinkled as he looked down at his son.

What a story, Teddy thought. It was one of his fondest memories. Oh my goodness, the first time he ever did his laundry; now that was even funnier than the baking story. His first week at college, NTID, had been full of firsts. His dad had assured him that laundry cost twenty-five cents, and he could get detergent from a machine like at Colgate, where he had gone to college in the '50s. Teddy went to the laundry room with one dollar in his pockets, four quarters' worth, plus the laundry basket. He saw two other students in the basement doing their own laundry, so he looked around for the detergent dispenser. Uh-oh, there was not one there.

"Hey, dude -- is there a detergent machine here?" Teddy asked this other guy who was at one of the machines. He recognized him from his eighth floor group in Tower A. He seemed like a nice guy, approachable; his own height and physique, not intimidating for him to approach, as he was very shy. The name escaped him. Maybe Justin?

"Hey, is your name Justin?"

"Yes, my name is Justin. There is no detergent machine here. Who told you that?"

Teddy felt sheepish and stupid. "My dad, when he went to college twenty-five years ago, had that in his laundry room. It cost twenty-five cents!"

Justin guffawed and looked around the room. "This isn't the '50s anymore, kiddo! You are on your own. FYI, each load costs seventy-five cents, not twenty-five!" Shaking his head, he went back to taking clothes out of the washer and putting them in the dryer.

"Umm…is it possible to borrow yours and I will repay you the favor next time we meet?"

"If I am gonna give you my detergent, what is your name? You can call me JT for short. That is what the babes call me!" Justin grinned and his arm was outstretched with the Tide in his right hand. "Here you go! Next time, buy your own and let me use it."

Teddy laughed. "Thanks, JT. I do owe you one! Inflation!"

Those two were among the many stories Teddy had in his memory, adjusting to a life of independence away from home.

So, where was Luis? Definitely out planning the next move. He'd better get showered and dressed to go to the cafeteria for breakfast. It would be mobbed with students eagerly awaiting news about the next thing to do for the protest. Hurriedly showering, he did not waste any time lingering like he usually did. After getting dressed, he made sure he had his wallet and keys in his pockets; then he slammed the door of his room in Cogswell Hall, and ran down the stairs and outside. There were students walking to the cafeteria as if there was a faith healer in there. Hordes! He'd better hurry, or there would be no place to sit to eat.

Sure enough, there was a long line of students snaking outside Carlin Hall, which was very unusual because it was a Monday morning at 9 a.m. when all students were supposed to be in class. Teddy turned around looking for a familiar face. Ah, there was Tom! He had come to Gallaudet the same day as Teddy, so they met at orientation.

Tom was from New Jersey and had been mainstreamed his whole life, never attending a school for the deaf. He was not yet a good signer, but he had learned a lot in just two months after arriving. He was about the same height as Teddy, just more athletic and toned. He played intramural softball and was quite athletic, showing off his prowess with a Frisbee. Teddy wished he was more prolific at these kinds of things. Tom was adept even at camping, hiking, canoeing, and horseback riding.

Tom was dating a deaf woman, Bridget, who was really smart. Teddy had tried to ask Bridget out, but evidently she liked many of the same outdoors activities that Tom enjoyed, so that had been a dead-end for him. Teddy had wanted to date her also, but respected Tom for having approached her first, so he respected Tom's "first dibs" as a part of the guys' code — never go after your friend's girl!

"Hey, Tom — what is going on in there, anyway?" He could see

Tom's eyes wide open, which was a first. Since arriving at Gallaudet, Tom had been easygoing, and it looked like he was half asleep all the time. But not today! He always had been clean-shaven, which was ironic because he seemed like he was not even out of bed with his dozing-off facial expression. This was definitely a new day with Tom's face stubble, which Teddy had never seen before on him.

"Hey back at you, Teddy! Didn't you hear? They brought school buses over from MSSD and Kendall School to the gates and slashed the tires to block the entrances! Plus the student leaders have come up with four demands for the board to follow! This is so exciting for us!"

Slashed tires? Blocked entrances? Student demands? Was this the '60s at Columbia University? It felt like a time warp for Teddy. He had long read about the peaceniks who protested against Vietnam and the draft at many college campuses. Kent State had resulted in four student deaths at the hands of an undertrained, overeager National Guard unit which had fired upon unarmed college students who were merely protesting an unjust war started by politicians in their ivory tower. Surely, this could not be happening.

"You gotta be kidding, Tom! What are the demands?" Teddy could not wait to find out what the story was up to now.

"OK, Teddy, you better be sitting down for this. Oh, yeah – we are outside, so there's no place to sit. Ha ha! One, Zinser must resign and a deaf president be selected…"

"Tom, of course that would be number one!" Teddy's eyes rolled upward. That was too obvious for anyone who knew what was going on with the protest. People around them shoved and jostled for a position in line to get into the cafeteria for breakfast. Teddy could feel arms bumping into him, but he did not mind because he was obsessed with finding out the story.

"You want to know the other three demands, buddy? Shut up!" Tom barked. Oops. He had not meant to yell at Teddy, who was one of his best friends on campus. When he arrived at Gallaudet, he had been lost like a homeless dog in a shelter. Teddy had stuck by him through the first two months, even as he started dating Bridget.

"Sorry, Teddy. I am all wound up by what has been happening here last night and this morning!" Tom had this sheepish look on his face and he looked like he was fighting back tears. Not here, guy! There were too many students around them to cry like a little schoolkid! Facing, Teddy, he admonished himself to get a semblance of self-control before he went on to tell him more news.

Whoa, Tom is all uptight this morning, thought Teddy. Nice of him, though, to apologize to his face. He felt bad about having aggravated Tom's stress levels. Better let him finish, then ask more questions.

"Two, Spilman must resign from the board completely. Three, the percentage of deaf board members must go up to 51%. Four, there are to be no reprisals against any of the protestors!" Tom rattled off each demand on his fingers. "How about those for you, Teddy? What do you think? The leaders will give the board these demands at noon today when Spilman and her motley crew arrive on campus."

"Those are great demands, Tom! Do you think we can really attain those? It is a tall order!" Teddy was elated. What audacity from the student leaders! He had never heard of anything like this happening in the Deaf world before. Word would definitely get out on campus and beyond when people started using their TTYs. Funny how communications had changed over the past few decades for deaf people.

The old TTYs had been huge and clunky, like steel factory machines you would find on a car assembly line that Henry Ford built back in the 1920s, or even before then, for the Model-T. Paper had been expensive and the TTYs were extremely loud, which was a hassle for hearing people who lived in the same household. Now they had TTYs which were portable and could be carried under one arm, weighing less than eight pounds. What would people come up with in the future?

He had just started learning how to use the 5 ¼" floppy disks that were needed to save word processing on the new PC computers in the basement of the library where the lab was. It was really funny not having to use the correction ribbon or the special white-out that was needed to erase the inevitable mistakes that happened when someone typed. Thank God for his high school teacher who taught his typing class the summer before his senior year of high school.

Before that summer, Teddy had to look all over the keyboard to find each letter with an index finger, his tongue sticking out as he became more and more frustrated by the arduous task of typing. Plus, the class had no interpreter, as he was in a hearing school, so he had to look up at Mr. Davis, who lectured the class. But in four short weeks, thanks to Davis's taskmaster attitude, he had gone from twenty-five words a minute to eighty. Now he could type even without looking at the keyboard, memorizing the QWERTY locations of each letter.

This typing speed was so important for Teddy because of his frequent use of TTYs. Before he took this summer typing class, he took forever in replying on the TTY to anyone that he chatted with over the phone. The bill every month was in the hundreds of dollars. His parents had admonished him to take the typing class so he could cut down on phone minutes in each conversation. Once he reached eighty words per minute, the phone bill had gone down dramatically and his parents had been very happy to save so much money!

"Teddy, I think it is quite doable. Did you know that there was no deaf member on the board until 1947, over eighty years since Gallaudet's founding in 1864? Isn't that outrageous? There are only four deaf members out of twenty-one right now!" Tom had a disgusted look on his face as he peered around him.

Other students were starting to listen to their conversation, entranced by what they were discussing, especially the historical trivia that was being thrown around about Gallaudet. They knew that this information might prove to be useful in case reporters, family, or friends came to ask questions about what was going on -- background that was needed for more information on the protest.

Teddy gaped. "Are you kidding me? That is absolutely unbelievable. I had no idea... Where is everybody, anyway? Luis?" He thought of his roommate who had a no-holds-barred attitude about everything. Luis was one of those types who would be perfect for the Skulls and Bones, which was a secretive fraternity based at Yale University. The current vice president, George H. W. Bush, had been a member when he was in college there, and there were countless other prominent statesmen who had been involved in that organization. The same went for the deaf version of this type of society at Gallaudet: Kappa Gamma. He had heard a rumor that KG was seriously thinking of recruiting Luis as part of the next rushing class.

KG was a staple on campus, having been at Gallaudet since January of 1901. Teddy and Tom had pored over countless articles and other sources of information about KG and its sister sorority, Phi Kappa Zeta. KG was the oldest fraternity on campus, with an extremely long list of distinguished alumni who came through its ranks over the years.

Luis fit their description of an ideal candidate: fluent in ASL, educated in a school for the deaf, strong leadership skills, attendance at YLC, and an extremely likeable personality. As for Teddy himself, he doubted KG would be interested in him because he was a graduate student with no fluency in ASL and little background/experience with the Deaf world.

"Luis? Wow -- last I heard, he hot-wired three buses from MSSD and brought them to each of the three gates that are not on Florida Avenue! Plus his friends brought their cars and parked them at each of the two front entrances and locked the cars so nobody can drive them away, and slashed all of the tires. It was the most unbelievable thing I ever saw!" Tom guffawed and looked around him.

Other students erupted in cheers as they watched him sign what Luis had just done that morning. Luis was becoming well-known on campus for his daring exploits and reckless attitude. Although he was not a good student, he still managed to eke out a "C" average, thus staying on campus for the time being. Teddy wasn't sure if Luis would be able to keep up with the work due to his mediocre reading skills, but his personality was undeniably charismatic and energetic.

Jeez, that Luis was something else. His roommate! They were probably over at Chapel Hall meeting with faculty members and anyone who was in the administration. That made sense.

"So, the board is coming later today, Tom? That is a hopeful sign!"

Tom huffed, shaking his head. "Mark my words, Teddy. The board, with Spilman leading, won't easily agree to this — we better hunker down and stay for the long haul, even possibly miss spring break -- that's next week!"

Miss spring break? No way. Many people had plane tickets, hotel reservations for Cancun, Florida, or other warm places where college students typically spent their vacations during school. He chuckled, remembering his favorite movie, *Fraternity Vacation*, with that nerd, Wendell Tvidt, who went to Palm Springs with Mother and Joe who were his frat brothers.

Wendell's dad had promised Mother and Joe a brand new hot tub if they could "show his son a good time," winking as he said it. At the end, Wendell ended up winning a huge bet with the arrogant Chaz Lawlor III, who was the pride and joy of the rival fraternity at their college, sleeping with the gorgeous Ashley Taylor. Now that would be his dream vacation!

"Miss spring break? All of those students? Surely, you jest, Tom!" Teddy blinked nervously. Would all of these students give up their vacation and money? Now that would be something.

Teddy knew all about protests and how important it was to voice opinions in America, as this country was founded on a democracy. He was curious what Tom would say about protests in general and why Gallaudet students were willing to miss spring break to make the point of how important having a deaf president was.

"Tom, what do you tell people when they ask you why it is important to miss spring break for this protest?" Teddy asked.

Tom had studied political science in college, just like Teddy had. "Look at the history of protests in America. Our colonial forefathers had the ultimate protest against Great Britain and even went to war with their colonial oppressors. Look at African-Americans, women, and other groups. They all went to extremes to get their point across. Gandhi in India. Can you imagine how scared these people were, facing such superior firepower and resources on the other side?"

Teddy had not realized how powerful emotions could be in the face of oppression, especially if confronted with seemingly insurmountable odds. Would missing spring break actually make a difference to this movement? He wondered what students would be willing to do to prevail.

Teddy breathed in deeply for a moment. He understood now. "Let's go in and eat. We are gonna need our energy for today if we will be standing outside shouting and waving at cars that pass us by on Florida Avenue!" By now, the two of them were standing inside right at the entrance, where the person swiped ID cards for those on the meal plan.

"Second that, Teddy!" Tom exclaimed with a big smile on his face. He put his right arm around Teddy. They were buddies through and through in two short months of being on campus. Nothing was going to separate them. They had become blood brothers from their shared experience arriving on campus.

They went inside the cafeteria, jostled on by rowdy and excited students standing behind them in line. Even though Teddy could not hear anything inside the cafeteria, he could see how many faces there were with strong emotions on them. He also could imagine the noise bouncing off the walls with the mouth movements students were making with their screaming and yelling.

It was going to be a crazy day, for sure. Teddy did not know how accurate his prediction would be. After breakfast, he walked with a few others over to Kendall School where one of the gates was locked. It was right behind Clerc Hall, so it was only a five- minute stroll for the students.

Kendall School was where the elementary deaf kids went to classes during the day. It was a gorgeous brick building, very modern inside, with colorful carpets and many bulletin boards all over the walls.

It was a mob scene there! Teddy neared Kendall and could see there was a mob standing right near the gate. It was padlocked and there were a few security people trying to cut a hole in the chain link fence so that administrators and faculty could get access to campus. Luckily, he had arrived just when a black sedan arrived at the gate. His head darted about as he looked for a familiar face to find out what was going on. What was this? It felt like *The Twilight Zone*!

Was Howie here? There was David! He was dressed in army fatigues and black boots. That was him for sure. He had dreamed of being in the military his entire life and he had told Teddy a story about trying to enlist in his senior year of high school. Teddy could not believe it when David told him that story a month or so ago in the cafeteria. David said he went into the Army recruiting center one day after school and asked to join after graduation. They knew he was deaf from the hearing aids he was wearing and told him that he could not qualify on medical grounds. Deaf people cannot fight for their country? To Teddy, that was unfair.

"David! What is going on?" Teddy knew that David was hard of hearing, so he could yell and David would hear him. "Why is security here? Tell me what's happening!"

David slowly turned around with a serious look on his face. "Teddy! You won't believe this! Glad you are here to see this. One of the board members, a hearing guy, just left. Security told him he could be in physical danger if he tried to get on campus today. But a deaf member just went through the hole in the fence, escorted by campus security officers. Look!"

Teddy saw where David was pointing. There was the deaf board member, hugging his son who was among the protestors. What a moment to witness for Teddy. He wished he had a father that could sign and understand about Deaf pride. He had been lucky in one regard, that his parents had high expectations of him academically when he was growing up. But he was still lonely among his family.

Suddenly, his attention riveted on this guy standing on a car near the gate where the father and son had hugged just now. Who was this guy? He had a denim brown jacket, light blue jeans, and he looked familiar to Teddy. What was his name? He looked very angry. Teddy poked David and pointed his head toward the speaker.

"Do you know who that is, David?" Teddy still could not place him right away even though this guy was a familiar face on campus.

"Are you kidding me? That's Eric! He is a ladies' man and a really strong deaf individual here on campus. Let's listen to his speech. He always has something good to say!"

Their mouths were agape as Eric explained how a police tow truck driver hit him in the face when he tapped the driver on the shoulder to get his attention. Man, that was so wrong! Didn't cops know anything about Deaf culture or even have any common sense?

"David! How stupid was that cop driver anyway?" Teddy shook his head. Hopefully, there would be no incidents of violence. That would mar the protest which was in its infancy. He recognized many faces in the crowd who were attentively listening to Eric. Many of them had contorted expressions on their faces and they were obviously angry about what had happened. Luckily, Eric had not retaliated and when other cops arrived, they took the driver away without incident.

A few hours later, after mingling with the crowd of students at Kendall, Teddy was already tired. He was in Clerc Hall, sitting down with Rhonda in her small bedroom, debating the pros and cons of this protest. They sat on her twin bed, their legs overlapping each other's, as they were comfortable with each other as best friends.

To his great surprise, Rhonda was opposed to this entire movement. She was 100% behind Zinser's appointment. Teddy could not understand this. He became upset and suddenly stood up, pacing around her room. His feet followed the pattern on her rug which was multicolored and had always fascinated Teddy.

"Let's go out into the TV lounge, Rhonda," said Teddy. "I feel suffocated in here and I need room to breathe and think. That OK?"

Rhonda had a surprised look on her face. She had not wanted to upset Teddy whom she really liked a lot. They had met not long ago when they attended a party at a mutual friend's dorm room, and got to talking about their mutual interests. It turned out that she was from Long Island, the same as Teddy. They shared a new-found fluency in ASL.

Rhonda had learned from mingling on campus, arriving in January with basic vocabulary. Teddy had been much further along and Howie was the one who taught him ASL grammar and usage at the conversational level. Everything had been going smoothly, with them starting to like each other. Rhonda was seeing someone at Catholic University, a hearing guy with no sign skills, but she was slowly becoming close to Teddy as a possible future boyfriend for her.

"Rhonda! Why are you supportive of Zinser? She can't even sign, and has never met a deaf person before!" Teddy fidgeted on the sofa in the third floor lounge at Clerc. Rhonda was seated right across from him in a lumpy chair that she had taken from her dorm room down the hall. "I mean, how can you possibly like Zinser? She is Spilman's puppet. All she is missing are the lines drawn from the edges of her lips to her chin like Pinocchio and the wires from her arms to wooden sticks being controlled by others!"

Boy, was he disappointed in Rhonda. Now she wasn't looking so angelic and pretty to Teddy. He had put high hopes on possibly forming a romantic bond with her as boyfriend and girlfriend, but this dream was sinking faster than the *Titanic* on a fast downward spiral by the second. She was beautiful -- had a face like the Mona Lisa, with fair skin and wavy long black hair to her shoulders.

The only defect she had, if you could call it one, was a bump on her nose. She had told him the story of when a softball hit her in the face during her high school days. Due to the lack of money, she had not gotten it operated on yet, but she was planning to. She was a slender 5'4" and many guys on campus would look in her direction as she walked by.

"I think Zinser deserves a chance to prove herself. She is a rainmaker. Don't you know what that is? Isn't money an important qualification with such a prominent appointment? Don't you know about affirmative action and the minimum threshold policy?" Rhonda felt frustrated, especially with her not-so-fluent ASL skills at this point, even though it had been two months since she started using it every day all day. What would make Teddy understand her point of view?

Rainmaker? Minimum threshold policy? What the heck was that? Teddy had no idea. Obviously, Rhonda saw Teddy's blank expression and she plowed ahead to explain. "First off, let me start with the idea that law firms have rainmakers. Those are the attorneys that drum up new business and new clients, thus adding billable hours to the coffers. They are the most valuable part of a law firm because they add money to the business of practicing law. My dad is a lawyer and I learned all about that from him. Gallaudet needs serious cash in-flow, so she would bring that to this school!"

Rhonda took another breath and continued. "Affirmative action, you know what that is? Zinser would be the first woman president of Gallaudet. Doesn't she have all of the qualifications? She has a doctoral degree and also has been an administrator at the college level for many years. She was part of the corporate world and thus could bring in some serious money as president."

Teddy was dumbfounded. He had never heard of anything like the spiel coming out of Rhonda. "Wait a minute, you think Zinser is qualified? Let's go through the qualifications a bit. She does have a Ph.D. and she has experience as an administrator at the top level. I grant you that. But shouldn't she be able to sign, at a place like Gallaudet?"

Rhonda paused for a minute, collecting her thoughts. Was signing absolutely mandatory? She didn't think so. "Doesn't Gallaudet have interpreters for that purpose? She, after all, is now taking ASL classes and learning about deaf culture. Look at Jordan. He doesn't have her breadth of experience. Corson has never been a college administrator before."

Teddy vehemently disagreed. This was all wrong! Nothing could have such twisted logic as this argument from Rhonda. He was going to stand up for all of his friends and everyone in Clerc Hall with Rhonda, no matter how he felt about her.

"Now, wait a minute again — your so-called minimum threshold policy tells you that Zinser is more qualified than Jordan and Corson? I do not think so for a single second! All of them have doctorates. Experience as administrators. But Zinser cannot communicate with students. How would they perceive her? Is money truly more important than respect and communication?"

Rhonda struggled to put words together to make Teddy understand how wrong he was about ASL being more important than money. Wasn't money what made the world go around? "Teddy, FYI, Gallaudet needs a lot of money to keep running as a college for the deaf. Congress will not always give Gallaudet the funds it needs to continue. Zinser would be a huge asset in that way. Plus, she would attract more students because of endowment funds with scholarship money."

Teddy chewed on these words for a moment, but decided Rhonda's reasoning was seriously flawed. Even though Zinser drew money and students, would they like her at first and then hate her later? He definitely was wrong about Rhonda. No longer did he want to date her, or even be in the same room with her. He felt nauseous. How could he have been wrong about this girl all along? They had met the first week of school and ate dinners together every night. Rhonda was fast becoming fluent in ASL, which was really unusual, at least in Teddy's limited experience with hearing signers that he knew on campus.

Teddy had been enthralled by her. She even had many deaf friends around her all the time. She was so cute. He always felt lost when looking into her eyes. This was a girl that he really wanted to be with. But not now. Not anymore. No way! How could she even think that Zinser was the right person to lead a university of deaf students when she could not sign anything and had hardly met a deaf person before?

That would be like, for lack of a better example, an Orthodox Jew becoming president of Catholic University or Notre Dame. Could you imagine the outrage and protests that would happen from that? It would not be based on prejudice of any kind, but instead on what people wanted: a leader like themselves. Gallaudet had gone way too many years being led by hearing men who either did not sign or had mediocre signing skills.

Listening to her, he felt like he was having an out-of-body experience. What rubbish she was throwing at him, supporting Zinser. Surely, this was sacrilege! How could anyone not want a deaf president? It had been 124 years and nobody in the president's house had been deaf. Just like America, 200+ years of existence, no women presidents. That was also a crime. It just wasn't right. Oppression and paternalism had to end now. He didn't want to talk with Rhonda anymore.

Her argument about money trumping sign language fluency brought raw emotions to the surface for Teddy. He had grown up being shunned in a hearing family. When he was only seven years old, he was thrust from a school for the deaf where he was comfortable among friends who he could communicate with. Then, he was thrown into a mainstream school setting from second grade until his high school graduation. He had seen his social development frozen for ten years, and when he graduated high school, he was only seven years old, if anyone looked at his emotional maturity.

"Listen, I am gonna leave. I don't feel good and I want to see what's going on. Talk later." He got up abruptly, surprising Rhonda with the quickness of his movement. She did not understand what was bothering him so much. *Better let her go, buddy,* Teddy said to himself. Wait until he told everyone about Rhonda's stance!

Rhonda was not going to last long on this campus, and he would make sure of that. He was angry at her. All that time together and she was like the fox in the henhouse, just like his family had been -- and that also was true of his nonsigning friends whom he threw out of his life when he went to NTID. He just could not take this anymore.

"Goodbye," he whispered to Rhonda. That was the end of his dream with her. He could not be with her anymore. Ever. Another dead end. It was just too bad. Let that other guy at Catholic University have her. He felt sick to his stomach, having been "rejected" yet again.

It brought memories back of when he played golf with his father. One day during the summer before he came to Gallaudet, his dad had shared a story with him that had stuck with him ever since. It had happened at a golf course on Long Island near their home and they were sitting on a golf cart on the fourth hole. How details like that could cement themselves in Teddy's mind, he could never understand. But they had and he would not forget them.

"Son, I have something I want to share with you." Dad was obviously not feeling at ease. He spoke and did not sign, as he and Mom never had taken a sign language course to communicate with him except for a couple of ASL classes they took in the continuing education program at the Lexington School for the Deaf. He took a deep breath and looked down at his golf shoes. His hands remained on his lap and slowly his eyes glided up to Teddy's face. He did not look very happy, which was unusual because he rarely showed any emotion on his face.

"I grew up always wanting to play golf with my father, your grand-father…" His eyes moistened as he took another deep breath. Teddy was flabbergasted. Was his father actually at a loss for words, strug-gling not to cry, right in front of him? Nobody was going to believe him if he ever told anyone what happened today. In fact, he doubted if anyone had ever seen his dad cry, not once, not ever. This ought to be good. If it brought his dad to this emotional state, then it was some-thing very painful and momentous in his own life.

"I am sorry, but please let me continue. I always asked my father if he wanted to go out and play golf with me. For many different reasons, he never quite had the time for that with me. I kept asking him for years, but he was busy winning trophies at his country club. Perform-ing surgeries at the hospital. As you know, he was chief of surgery at the time he passed away of a heart attack. He never stopped work-ing in his lifetime. He never showed me any interest in playing golf." Looking visibly relieved, his dad was suddenly quiet and shrugged his shoulders.

"Aw, Dad. That is really sad. But I am glad we get to play golf. It is always fun with you! We both have a lot of good memories. Do you re-member that time I almost got a hole-in-one at Bethpage on that pond hole? That lake had been my nemesis for four years when I was practic-ing with the golf team every week. If I had a dollar for every golf ball I hit into that damn lake, I would have retired already!" Teddy's eyes rolled upward as he shook his head ruefully. Dad chuckled and put his left arm around Teddy's shoulders.

Shaking off this memory of his dad and golf, he went running to Ely Center, where he saw that there were many students mingling. It was almost noon now. There was Howard! "Hey there — what's going on now?" Howie, as he called him, was his best friend on campus. He was a little crazy, but he was fun. All 6'2" of him, 220 pounds – grew up in a deaf family, deaf parents, went to VSDB at Staunton.

If anyone could understand this protest, it was Howie. He was such a character! They had become addicted to the PC video game, DOOM, in Teddy's private dorm room at Carlin Hall. Thanks to his advanced standing due to having a BA degree, he had gotten first priority in the dorm lottery, which made him a wanted man for a roommate. Lucky Luis had won a room with him, and it was all just pure luck. Howie wished he and Teddy could be roommates.

"Hey Teddy. I heard that ten student leaders, two faculty, and two staff members are meeting with the board and Spilman at noon. We should find out soon what's going on. Where did you just come from, and why are you out of breath?" Howie had an inquisitive look on his face, staring at Teddy. Teddy thought he better tell Howie about Rhonda. Howie had never liked her and this had eaten away at Teddy, but it looked like Howie was right on the money about her all along.

"I just came from arguing with Rhonda." Howie's eyes lit up and he had a knowing smile on his face. "She supports Zinser's appointment. Can you believe it? What a Benedict Arnold she is. I felt so sick at Clerc Hall, trading barbs with her in the TV lounge. I felt numb to the core. This was the girl that I had a serious crush on all these weeks here on campus! Who would have thought she felt this way?"

"Sorry, man. That must suck, finding out the girl of your dreams felt this way about deaf culture, Zinser, the board, Spilman." Howie's face softened as he felt bad for his best friend. Teddy deserved better and Howie had always felt that way ever since they first met when Teddy roamed around the library looking like he had lost his best friend. His face expression had been one of panic and it was obvious he was a newbie on campus.

Howie was a sophomore, so he had been around over a year and a half. He could not wait to become a junior and show those freshman girls a thing or two. He really had a high respect for Teddy's encyclopedic knowledge and fluent English skills. On more than one occasion, he had asked Teddy to help him with math, which was his stumbling block due to a learning disability he had since grade school in Virginia. He was in awe of Teddy taking pre-calculus and first-year calculus in a public high school without an interpreter. He knew that Teddy was profoundly deaf and that could not have been easy at all to accomplish.

But this Rhonda attitude he just could not fathom. Why would she oppose the protest? Didn't she want the president of Gallaudet to reflect who the students were? This was paternalism and oppression, pure and simple. If that was how Rhonda felt, then to hell with her. He would help Teddy find a better gal who was "deaf-friendly."

Parties abounded on campus. The Rock Festival every year in May was the best one of the year and it would be coming in just a month or so, provided this protest did not last that long. Now that would be a shame. Thousands of deaf students crammed into a small space, listening to rock music and their bodies gyrating, drinking. That was a heck of a party to look forward to! Not to worry -- he would give Teddy a real introduction to the campus life now that he was unstuck on that uppity hearing girl Rhonda.

"Hey, Teddy boy. Let's get a drink at the Rathskellar and we can forget our problems for a while. How about it?" Howie grinned and playfully shoved Teddy on the left shoulder.

Teddy's lips curled into a faint smile. He appreciated having such a good buddy in Howie. Howie was never down on himself. Somehow, he would be the positive vibe in the room and influence everyone else. There were so many memories of him and Howie in just two months of being friends. Teddy's sign skills had leapfrogged in just a short time because of Howie who was a fluent signer, coming from a deaf family.

Teddy had used simultaneous communication (SimCom) and Pidgin Signed English since he was a teenager, attending a teen club for the deaf on Long Island every other Friday, but he was shifting to American Sign Language which was the natural, God-given language of the deaf community -- not that fake, artificial manually coded English which had a plethora of names like MCE, SEE, PSE. Those were for deaf culture wannabes. Howie was going to make sure that Teddy came over to the ASL camp, and that was where he belonged. It was sad too that King Jordan, one of the two deaf finalists for the presidential job, used SimCom -- and he was a terrible signer, at that!

Teddy chuckled at the thought of becoming an ASL fluent signer. It would be all because of good ol' Howie! "Sure, man. Let's go to the Rat. Get some chow in our stomachs and await the decision of the board. It should be crawling with lovelies, so I can forget that whatshername stuck-up broad that I just wasted my time arguing with!"

"That's the spirit, Teddy! Off we go, on the yellow brick road!" Howie felt better, knowing that Teddy's spirits were raised just by being with him. Howie had not had many friends during his freshman year on campus. He admittedly was a little off-putting for many people. He was an absolute slob and often said the wrong things to people on campus. He did not mean to say them, but he lacked impulse control. Sort of like Tourette's, but a much milder form of it. He knew he had to get a grasp on it before graduating or he would never find a job nor get married. Teddy showed him enormous patience and good-naturedly would tease him about the things he came out with. It made for many hilarious moments for the two good friends.

He could remember the previous week when they went to Laurel Racetrack. Now that had been really memorable. On Friday, having no classes, they had gone to a local newspaper store and found a copy of the Daily Racing Form. Having no idea what to do in terms of handicapping, they looked through the huge amount of data on each race and decided to drive in Teddy's Honda Hatchback to Laurel, which was only thirty minutes away. To make a long story short, Teddy had come out $10 ahead while Howie lost $80 due to huge bets toward the end. Teddy was very conservative and was happy to just cover his costs.

Teddy laughed. That was their vintage humor. They always referred to movies, especially classics like *The Wizard of Oz,* to make a point when talking to people. Teddy had seen *Oz* many times and loved it, especially the part where the Wicked Witch melted into nothingness because of a mere bucket of water. And those winged monkeys! He had been scared of them when he watched the movie as a little kid. He had crouched behind the sofa whenever that big crystal ball appeared and the Witch summoned the leader of the monkeys to go after Dorothy and her crew who were on their way to Oz.

As he got older, he saw that the monkeys were comical and not scary at all. Perhaps that would happen with the board and Spilman, who reminded him of the Wizard hiding behind a curtain, appearing and sounding scary to everyone. In reality, she perhaps was a figure who had no real power and just looked bigger than she really was.

Soon the curtain would be opened, and everyone would see that woman for what she really was. Teddy was learning more and more about this woman who had run the board for years and could not sign a single word. It was offensive to him that people at Gallaudet and everywhere had accepted this status quo, but no more. He could see that students were very angry about Zinser's selection and he was very glad.

Was money really more important than having a president who signed and established a rapport with students? Was Rhonda actually right? Teddy refused even to debate the issue with himself. He was very upset. Wasn't this the elephant in the room, so to speak? People always debated about the importance of money in higher education. Was merit the most important factor, or was money? But at what price? He felt that this Zinser appointment had gone too far. Satisfied with his analysis of the issue, he returned to the present.

The Rat, what a place! It was the central pub of the campus where everyone came to eat, drink, and mingle. There was a huge TV screen on the wall that loomed on your left when you came through the white doors. Hearing people often commented to Teddy that they were shocked at how loud it was, considering most of the people there were deaf.

Graduate students went there to practice signing because they could not hear anyone talking, so they were forced to focus on other signers' hands and facial expressions to understand anything. It was even better than ear plugs because you could not stop the really loud noise, whereas you could just take the ear plugs out if you got tired of using your eyes for receptive practice.

He could see a few of his classmates in the Rat. "Hey, Mimi! What's up?" He saw her sitting at a booth with her new boyfriend Randy.

She was very cute and had not known any signs when she came onto campus that previous fall, one semester before him. Amazingly, in just a few months, she was almost fluent in ASL because of Randy. Mimi, whose full name was Monique, came from Maryland, grew up in a well-off family, and decided to become a teacher of the deaf. As she was hearing, she looked for a deaf boyfriend the very first day she arrived on campus. She and her best friend Melinda found two guys in the bookstore when they lined up with their stack of graduate school textbooks.

M&M, as everyone called Mimi and Melinda, had tittered and ogled these two really cute boys who turned out to be freshmen, perfect for their purpose because these guys would not be serious about a long-term relationship. But they definitely enjoyed the attention of two very pretty hearing grad students, and of course they had the horndog factor which satisfied certain needs that they had. The four of them started hanging out together. In fact, it was really funny because the two guys also had the same first initial, R. Richie and Randy, R&R. Rest and Recreation, that was the sign above their door in Krug Hall, and they always had parties going on in there. M&M were sure getting a crash course in the deaf culture from day one.

Melinda was definitely OCD, as she dressed to the nines. She spent an hour or more every night planning her entire outfit from head to toe. The colors had to match or else. Even her lipstick, nail polish, and socks were included in the repertoire. Teddy laughed every morning as he saw her walk into class. He had never seen anything like her before. He would not mind dating her though, even if she was high maintenance. God only knew how many purses she had, and pairs of shoes. It was a wonder that she had enough room in her dorm space for everything. Poor Veronica, having to be her roommate.

Richie sure did not mind, as they had been dating for a few months already and he was the type to wear polo shirts, matching pants, and loafers so they were a pretty good match to begin with. Everyone was starting to think Melinda and Richie would end up getting married in spite of the four years' difference in their ages. But Teddy didn't think that would happen. It was a gut feeling.

His hunches often paid off, as he had a sixth sense about these things. Even though he had never had a girlfriend before, he would see friends who were paired off into couples and he could somehow see who was compatible and who wasn't. Mimi was the total opposite, down to earth, easygoing, low maintenance. He wished he had met Mimi first before Randy, so he would have had a prayer. But it was not to be. Just as well.

"Hey, Teddy! How you doin'?" smiled Mimi. She winked at him and Randy waved hello. He was wearing a yellow t-shirt with that smiley face on it. Mimi, as usual, had some t-shirt and a sweater on. She was so pretty! Maybe one day she would break up with Randy and date him.

Teddy grinned and walked over to Mimi. He bent down and gave her a hug. She wrapped her arms around him. Mmmm, she smelled nice that day. Lucky Randy! "So, what have you heard about this entire protest so far?" asked Teddy.

"Not a lot. Randy, you hear anything yet?" Mimi looked at her boyfriend, who never ceased to cause her heart to flutter. He was so handsome, even though he was dressed in a t-shirt and jeans, and battered sneakers. But would she end up marrying him? Extremely doubtful. Now, that Teddy. He was much more her type and maybe she would give him a chance later when she grew tired of Randy. Not yet though. She did want to stay friends with Teddy and keep the door open for the future. He was very cute, shy and awkward around girls, which appealed to her.

She had even talked to her parents about this whole situation with Randy and Teddy. Her folks had subtly encouraged her to start thinking long-term and Teddy obviously was the better bet, as he was going to be a teacher just like her and they would have the summers off together. He also was more intelligent and had a great sense of humor, which he had gotten from his all-hearing family. Teddy's background appealed to her. She was hoping that no other female students became attracted to Teddy before she broke up with Randy, but that was something she couldn't control.

Randy looked up at Teddy and shrugged. What did he know, anyway? He was just a freshman and still did not have an ear to the ground on campus yet. He was still feeling his way around even though he was a popular student along with Richie, the other half of R&R. Dating Mimi was the best thing he had ever done. She had introduced him to a whole new world of hearing students who were learning how to sign. Having attended a school for the deaf in Texas, he took it for granted that all signers were deaf and native. Now he was getting a whole new outlook watching M&M learn ASL with classmates from all over the country who wanted to become teachers.

That Teddy was going to become a thorn in his side. Randy wanted to hold onto Mimi, but this deaf friend of hers who took classes with her could become a threat later on. But Randy forced himself to be nice to Mimi so he could stay on her good side and they would stay together for now. What did he care about Teddy? He mused on what to say to Mimi and Teddy; then he decided that diplomacy was the word of the day.

"Hiya Teddy. Haven't heard much yet. But there is supposed to be a rally in the gym today when the board finishes its meeting with the protest leaders. I am hoping word will get out as soon as the meeting ends. Is that what you heard also?"

As if Teddy would know, Randy mused. Teddy was buried in his books, studying for his graduate degree. Taking classes with hearing students at Gallaudet? He scoffed at the thought. What irony. Teddy had taken classes his entire life without an interpreter, then graduated from NTID/RIT using interpreters and now he was at Gallaudet taking classes among all hearing students? That was a laugh. He was such a bookworm, and he dismissed the thought that Mimi could ever be attracted to him.

But then again, who could figure out women these days? He wasn't exactly the boy next door that a gal would want to introduce to her parents. So anything could happen. Plus Teddy came over to Mimi's room on practically a daily basis. Every time he went to visit her, Teddy was either in the room or hanging around on the floor. He knew Teddy had no interest in any of the other girls, so it had to be Mimi. No question about it.

Teddy could sense Randy's hostility. Maybe it was just his imagination. Teddy envied Randy sitting right next to Mimi. He wished it was him sitting there. "Hey, do you guys remember Howie? Howie, Randy. Randy, Howie. You remember Mimi, right?" Teddy took a quick glance at Howie who was staring at Randy, daggers right at him. Oh jeez, Howie didn't like Randy much, did he? Better get Howie outta there. He had a tendency to get into scuffles at the slightest provocation.

"Hey, Howie, Let's grab a table over there!" Teddy pointed to an empty booth out of the sightline of Randy and Mimi. Anything to avoid being tempted to stare at this pretty girl! Finally taking his eyes off Mimi, Teddy turned around and forced his feet to step in front of one another until he arrived at the booth then he dumped himself onto the bench facing the opposite direction. Jeez! That was some situation he had defused back there.

Howie slumped into the bench opposite of him. Howie's hands were clenched into fists and slowly his hands opened up. He took a deep breath in and out.

Their eyes met across the table. Teddy began to laugh and Howie couldn't help but join in. Their laughter grew louder and louder until their eyes began to water. Teddy had tears rolling down his cheeks and he was convulsed in spasms from laughing so hard.

"Man, you are unbelievable! I thought you were going to punch Randy," exclaimed Teddy. "You really didn't like him back there, did you?"

"Good lord, no. He is a sneaky one, that guy. No good for Mimi!" sneered Howie. "One day, she will realize that and maybe you will have a chance."

Teddy beamed at this bonding moment – his best friend's sincere wish for him. He nodded sagely, agreeing with him. But right now, the main focus was finding out about the protest and updates. All of a sudden, a group came rushing into the Rat. Something was happening! Better find out! He could see some of the new students signing. That could not be -- looked like the board was holding fast and not accepting the protest's four demands that he had learned about this morning waiting in line for breakfast. That was not good. It could only mean trouble.

"Hey!" Teddy yelled. "What is going on over there?" He signed also to get someone to respond.

One of the students looked at him and shook his head. "Someone came out of the meeting just a few minutes ago. Spilman! She had her arms crossed on her torso, wearing that same dark jacket from last night. Her face was like a rock and she was definitely not gonna give in to us. There is a meeting at the gym at 3:00 this afternoon. Pass the word on!"

Meeting at the gym? That was a huge place! But it probably could not fit all 1,000+ students at Gallaudet if everyone showed up. He had no doubt that just about everyone would. Except Rhonda. She was the foremost on his mind even though she had disappointed him this morning. She had disappointed him with her obstinate support of paternalism and oppression. This caused him the same feeling of sorrow that he had fought against his entire childhood. To support Zinser was equivalent of his parents picking a mainstream school where he was ostracized and rejected.

Howie rubbed his hands with glee. "Oh, man! That means we are going to have quite the week! I told you this would happen if Zinser was picked. This is a once-in-a-lifetime event. We will never see anything like this again. Hey did you hear we are in the newspapers now?"

Teddy's mouth hung out. "Really? Did you see the papers already? What are they saying? Wanna go see what we can find in the bookstore?"

"Sure! Let's eat then run down there. Maybe Riggs Bank is open and we can clean out the newspapers, save them for your scrapbook of Gallaudet memories!"

Teddy laughed at Howie's comment about the scrapbook. But it was an idea that was starting to form in his mind already at this early stage, the first full day of whatever this turned out to be. If Gallaudet students were actually in _The Washington Post_, then this scrapbook idea was something to hold onto and germinate. It would be very useful for future memories, especially if he were to become a social studies teacher of the deaf. Primary sources were always good to have, even if they wrote a book chronicling these events later on.

Later, they ambled down the stairs and upon entering the basement area, they looked to their right where the bookstore was. It was mobbed with people trying to get a copy of _The Washington Post_!

"Howie, let's grab a copy too! It will be a collector's item. _USA TODAY_ also!" They made a beeline for the newspaper stand and both were lucky to get one copy of each. Waiting in line, they recognized many faces from classes and the cafeteria. Everyone was buzzing about the upcoming gym rally to be held later. "Spilman…" "Board…" "Protest…" They could only snatch a word here and there with all those arms flailing around them, so they hurriedly paid for the newspapers and ran back outside into the common area. Spotting an open bench in the bowling area, Teddy grabbed Howie's shirt and pulled him toward it.

"C'mon, let's go over there and read the papers! Nobody is sitting there for whatever reason," Teddy said. This ought to be good. How much could the newspapers have found out in a short time since last night?

Oh. My. God. Was he wrong! It was already front page news! *USA TODAY* screamed: "Deaf students boycott university" with the subheading "Officials: new head will stay." This was the primetime! *The Washington Post* also had a headline: Students Close Gallaudet U.: Protesters Demand a Deaf President.

Teddy wondered what *The New York Times* and other newspapers had to say. Probably more of the same thing. Amazing. He would never have believed this would happen. The only thing that would surprise him more would be one of two things: a terrorist attack on the United States, and a president of color in the White House. Would those things happen in his lifetime? he wondered. Plus Jesus's return, if he was indeed the Messiah that all of those Christians believed. Now that was quite a bunch of memories he wished he didn't have.

When he was a freshman at NTID/RIT, his roommate had been a Bible-thumping Christian who belonged to a fundamentalist church in Rochester. One day, he had happened to see a comic book on his roommate Bobby's desk entitled: "Alberto." Since he had loved to read comic books as a kid growing up without captions, he picked it up and went over to his desk to start reading. Big mistake. He became enthralled by the story of a former Catholic priest who had delved into the "dark history" of the Church and railed against its teachings which were against the Bible.

Jesus? Who was that? Teddy had no idea. He did remember one afternoon when he was in elementary school, sixth grade probably, when he and his mother went to the mall to get a gift for someone. Walking back to the car, he found someone shoving a tract in front of him. "See You Later. Where?" He could remember that like it was yesterday. He had asked his mother what this was and she grabbed it, throwing it aside like it was contagious. He remembered seeing a figure on back, dressed in a robe, with beard and long hair on his face.

For Teddy, reading "Alberto" had been the beginning of years of going to churches and trying to find out answers to his questions about life, where he was going after he died, the validity of the Catholic religion. Answers never came so he had given up on this quest. That would really have been something, Jesus's return. This protest was the second best thing. Very exciting!

Seeing more and more students mingling in the common area, they got up and started sharing tidbits of information from the newspapers for a while. Time flew by and before they knew it, the clock read three o'clock. They had better get over to the gym quickly before it became overcrowded with students from all over campus!

Sure enough, it was mobbed by the time the two of them got there. It took ten minutes to squeeze through the doors, and finally they were in the gym. Every seat was taken! So they had to sit on the wooden floor, but that did not matter. They were in there. Spilman was standing at the podium with an interpreter standing on her right. It was the same one from the night before, Teddy noted. He recognized her from the Mayflower Hotel.

That poor woman. What did she do in her previous life to deserve all that scorn being heaped on Spilman through her? He hoped she was getting paid a lot of money for this! He bet she would be, as she was at the hotel late the night before and all that day at Gallaudet. At least she got something out of this, plus the memories and stories she would get to tell one day. She had to stand there resolute and quiet while everyone around her was throwing insults and taunts at Spilman. Not a fun experience.

Spilman was obviously nervous. She paced around the podium, never going in front of it to expose herself to the angry crowd that was watching her every move. The board was seated behind her in two rows, looking straight ahead. What an interesting thing -- they were almost all hearing, and only a few of them could sign. That was a sad reflection of the way things had been all these years, but Teddy doubted this would continue, as a result of this protest which was growing bigger by the hour.

It was time! Spilman approached the microphone on the podium and tapped it tentatively with her right index finger. She looked behind her at the board sitting down and then turned around straight ahead to start speaking to the crowd which was filling up the gym to its capacity. There were people standing all along the walls, as every sitting space was already occupied.

Teddy's eyes were riveted by a solitary figure which made its way up the steps to Spilman's back left. This person walked quickly in front of the interpreter and he waved his arms frantically. What was this? Teddy's mouth was wide open. Now what? Was this a protestor? A member of the board? A disgruntled faculty member? Or some crazy stranger off the street?

This figure was not very imposing at all. He had black hair, a mustache, tan jacket. He wore a dark polo shirt, jeans, white sneakers. But his demeanor gave away his stature and Teddy started to recognize his face. Wasn't that Harvey Goodstein? Why was he standing there like that?

"Everyone!" signed Goodstein. "The board has steadfastly refused to even listen to our demands. There is no use in wasting our time listening to Spilman's spiel here. Let's all walk out and show her we mean business! Let's go!" He swiveled around and hurried down the steps. Seated people made a wide path for him to walk through to the front doors. Spilman was apoplectic, not being able to utter a word. The interpreter, poor woman, didn't know what to do either.

Fire alarms abruptly started blaring. There was a lot of shouting among the people in the crowd. Spilman had a look of fury on her face. She thundered, "We are not going to hear you if you scream so loudly that we can't have a dialogue!" As the interpreter signed what she said, students started laughing at the board members seated on the platform.

Reactions were universal. One student signed, "What noise? Why not sign for yourself? If you signed, we could hear you!" The interpreter's face went white as she signed that back to Spilman, who became quiet, looking around her. This was just like the Mayflower Hotel. Her expression became flat and her hands dropped to her sides. There was just no use in arguing with this crowd today. It was up to the entire board to decide what to do. The four demands were ludicrous, and Zinser's selection was final.

Suddenly, people who were previously seated both on the floor and in the bleachers got up and crowded toward the front doors. Spilman started waving her arms just like Goodstein had done, to no avail. Nobody was paying attention to her. Teddy himself got up and so did Howie. Ignoring the president of the Gallaudet board? That was really big. There was no way this protest was going away quietly. Where was everyone going?

Word got around that they were marching to the Capitol. Of what? The whole country? Teddy didn't believe it. He had been to the Capitol several times as a sightseeing tourist. How could all these people flock to our nation's capital and mass in front of the building where the American senators and representatives met?

The last time he had been there was with Howie at 1 a.m. to watch senators debate the latest budget numbers. They had gone through security without a hitch and they had sat down in the senate chambers.

What a thrill it had been to see Edward Kennedy stand and orate to the other senators! He was, in fact, named after Senator Kennedy. He had been born less than a year after JFK was shot. His parents, Jack and Elise, had thought about the name John or Jack, but to them this was going to be too common. The same went for Robert.

They thought the next president was going to be Teddy, so they figured why not name their son after a Kennedy? His last name was Rose Fitzgerald Kennedy's maiden name before she married Joseph Kennedy, Sr. He had sat there for thirty minutes watching his namesake debate with the other senators until Howie nudged him in the ribs and said they should get going.

Onward to the Capitol it was for them! Howie and he walked to the front gates where the security booth was. Only twelve hours ago, he had stepped off the precipice onto the street as one of the first few students to block traffic and stand up for a deaf president. This had changed his life forever. Was it only twelve hours? It seemed like a lifetime to Teddy. Howie knew the significance of the moment, as he had arrived there just in time to see Teddy make that momentous decision to become actively involved in the protest last night. They continued walking down 8th Avenue with everyone else and continued to march toward the Capitol.

Who was going to speak there? Wouldn't the Capitol police force want to block everyone from getting there en masse? Now they were walking in the middle of traffic! Drivers honked their horns, but they had smiles on their faces. Obviously, word had gotten out through the news about what was happening at Gallaudet. DC cops halted traffic as the many students walked through intersections and weaved in and out between cars that were stalled in the street. It was like what you would see on an ant farm, with so many moving creatures going in the same direction.

So this was what it would have been like to watch Martin Luther

King, Jr.'s "I have a dream" speech that day in August of 1963 with over 200,000 supporters lined up at the steps of the Lincoln Memorial. The weather, just like that day back in 1963, was sunny and warm. It was like the clouds had parted for the sun to shine on them as they flocked to the Capitol.

Teddy could see the Lincoln Memorial across the Washington Mall. The Reflecting Pool water glistened and rippled all the way from the Capitol to the Lincoln Memorial. It could not have been a prettier day for this kind of event, mused Teddy. Someone upstairs evidently approved. Good thing it had not been raining and cold. What would the turnout have been then? A moot question, as the temperatures were very warm for a March afternoon.

Now they were at the steps of the Capitol, anticipating speeches by various deaf leaders. Jeff Rosen! Gary Olsen! There were so many of them up there, including the four deaf student leaders who had met with the board. He could recognize their faces as they looked over the ever-swelling crowd. He could see banners and signs. His favorite one was "We Won't Give Up ... Until We Have a Deaf President!" There was an impromptu wave going across back and forth, and Teddy joined in along with Howie. This was momentous! The whole world's eyes were upon them. They were not going anywhere, that was for sure.

News vans! He could see them parking right near them on the side streets. Reporters were hurrying to get their equipment together and huddling with camera people who set up their video camcorders to record this event for the news. Where were his classmates? They had to be here somewhere, but it was nearly impossible to find anyone in this sea of faces.

There were people of all ages and races -- just amazing. Suddenly, the wave stopped and all eyes looked at the top of the steps. It looked like the famous Philadelphia steps where Sly Stallone had run up to the top and raised his outstretched arms for the Rocky movie. Perhaps they were like that underdog against the proverbial favorite Apollo

Creed, which was Spilman and the board of trustees.

An amazing afternoon it was. Everyone's heart was filled with pride and joy at having shown their unity in the face of seemingly-insurmountable odds. They were individually neither important nor powerful, but as a growing crowd, they were like a tidal wave that was heading toward the dam with the word "PATERNALISM" written across it. Upon getting back to the front entrance, Teddy was surprised to see even more people standing on the sidewalk and all over the front entrance with signs and banners proclaiming DEAF PRESIDENT NOW! and HONK FOR A DEAF PREZ!

Cars and trucks were whizzing by, and he could hear the honking as the drivers gave them a thumbs-up sign, showing solidarity with a university they had never set foot on. He bet that nobody had even given Gallaudet a second thought prior to this day, and now they knew who these students were in the midst of their own neighborhood! There were even more news vans parked on campus, one long line facing Benson Hall, with students mingling around reporters.

He noticed something new: there were some people who had colored armbands on their sleeves. What was up with that? Walking closer to the campus, he realized that these were obviously interpreters who were helping reporters communicate with protestors to get their views and stories for the newspapers. That was a great idea! What would they think of next? Where were these interpreters coming from?

"Howie, do you see the people with colored armbands?" Teddy pointed at several of them as they walked through the front entrance, squeezing through the multitude.

"Yeah! They must be interpreters! Did I ever tell you that joke about the French guy, the Russian guy, and Deaf American guy on the train?" Howie snickered.

That Howie and his jokes! Teddy knew many of them by heart, as he had watched Howie relate these silly jokes to anyone he met. "Yes, that one I remember!" As if he could forget. The way the joke went was this: on a train, three deaf guys meet. The French guy opens the window and throws out expensive paintings, saying, "It is only art, we have plenty of it back home in Paris."

The deaf Russian throws out vodka through the window, saying, "We have plenty of vodka in Moscow to drink." The American calls for an interpreter and when one arrives, he throws that poor interpreter out the window. The Frenchman and Russian are shocked, asking why he did that. He says, "There are plenty of interpreters in America!"

Reporters looked for anyone to talk to, so they could get their stories in on time. Two of them approached Teddy. One of them asked him, "What are your feelings about this, young man?" An interpreter signed to him for the reporter. Teddy felt important. Finally he was going to be able to say what was on his mind, after twenty-four years of being quiet in an all-hearing family, relegated to the background.

"You want to know how I feel? After all these years of feeling like a second-class citizen in my family and at my public schools I attended growing up, it is liberating to be standing here, feeling vindicated that the emotions I had were all legitimate. I feel like I am at MLK's speech in 1963 at the Lincoln Memorial..."

The reporter listened to the interpreter and her face was enraptured by what Teddy was saying. "By the way, my name is Teddy Fitzgerald. I grew up oral and did not know any sign language until I was a junior in high school. It was very frustrating not being able to participate in family meals. I saw my two younger sisters chat with my parents and each other so easily. It got to the point where I became very angry and broke the family rule of staying until the end of the meal...are you sure you want to listen to this?"

Teddy stole a look at the reporter. She was still staring at him, even as she listened to the interpreter voice for him.

"Yes, definitely...that's why we are here. To get your story and the stories of the other students who felt strongly enough to make a stand here!" She raised her microphone and waved it in the interpreter's face. "Go on!"

Teddy felt empowered, and continued. "I almost went to a regular university, but ended up at NTID/RIT. You know what that is and where, yes?" The reporter nodded at Teddy. "OK, I graduated from there in 1986 and then worked at the IRS for a while, but it was not what I wanted to do with my life. Then, I decided I wanted to become a teacher of the deaf, so I had to come to the Mecca of deaf culture, the Harvard of deaf schools, Gallaudet. Now this happens, a hearing president who cannot sign a single word. You can see why I am so angry, disappointed with the board's choice!"

The reporter didn't realize Teddy was done; then she almost dropped her microphone as the last words from the interpreter's lips trailed off. She tucked the microphone under her left arm and clapped. "That was a wonderful commentary. What is your name again, Mister ... ?"

"Theodore Fitzgerald, known as Teddy. I was named after Senator Ted Kennedy and ironically enough, my last name is Rose Kennedy's maiden name. You can quote me on all of that." Teddy smiled as the reporter jotted that down in her notepad.

Howie, standing next to Teddy, marveled at his best friend's transformation from the day before. It was like Clark Kent turning into Superman! Growing up, Howie had been hooked on Action! Comics and anything related to Superman. His favorite movie moment had been in the Superman comic where he had lost his superpowers to Lex Luthor as a result of treachery at the Fortress of Solitude up in Alaska where Luthor had nabbed his one true love, Lois Lane. In return for her safety, he had given up his superhuman powers, but later on, he regained them by fooling Luthor in return. Then, when he went back to a diner where he had been punched by a brash-talking customer with Lois Lane standing beside him, he found that same guy and threw him across the long dining table. Everyone asked him how he did that and he replied, "I worked out a little!"

This was the same feeling he had watching Teddy answer to the reporter about his experiences growing up. Teddy's posture became more and more confident and his signing was almost pure ASL. How good was that? Since January, he had chatted with Teddy, gently correcting his signing so it would be more ASL. Now the world was witnessing Teddy sign ASL! There were students standing around him, Teddy, the reporter, and the interpreter. When Teddy was finished, there were many hands waving in the air in approval of what Teddy had told the reporter. It had been worth all that time and effort.

He did envy Teddy's fluency in English. He, Howard Jameson, had never been able to read at the same level as Teddy. Why was that? His parents never had been readers. Teddy had told him how he grew up reading Robert Ludlum and other authors. Teddy had been a bookworm as a mainstreamed student, while Howie was at a school for the deaf without any real impetus to read books. Teachers at Staunton had had low expectations for Howie and his classmates. Some teachers did not even sign that well, and very few could converse with students in ASL. It all added up to a very unfair disadvantage for Howie and other students who were unlucky enough to lack parents and other adults who enjoyed daily reading.

Once, he had witnessed Teddy accept a bet from another student in Cogswell as they were all watching TV in the lounge on the second floor. The gullible student had never met Teddy before and he bet Teddy that there was no way anyone could read a certain book within three hours. Obviously, he had never met Teddy before.

To make a long story short, Teddy won the bet that he could read that book, and he even finished in two hours, not three! The student had asked Teddy a few questions about the story and Teddy answered them all correctly. It was an easy $5 for Teddy and another $5 for Howie. Never bet against a great reader like Teddy! Now with his ASL fluency on top of the excellent reading ability, there was no stopping Teddy.

"Hey, Teddy! That was a great interview you gave the reporter. Where did you find the words to express yourself so well?" Howie looked at Teddy with undisguised admiration. This guy was a winner, no doubt about it. He better stick to Teddy and they would go places in life. Other students crowded Teddy, congratulating him on expressing himself so well with his support of the protest. Rhonda could go jump off a cliff for all he and Teddy cared. It was good that Teddy was well rid of her for once and all.

"Thanks, Howie! Everyone! I feel liberated and proud that we are fighting for a just cause here with the protest. There's a new name for it: Deaf President Now, also known as DPN!" cheered Teddy.

The students who saw Teddy sign that also cheered. It was the birth of the DPN movement. As time crawled by that afternoon, faculty members started to join the swelling ranks and so did students from all over Gallaudet. Then, word trickled down from the leadership that the gates would open on Tuesday, but students were to boycott classes so the board would not be able to claim victory. There also would be a faculty-wide meeting to decide what to do about classes, homework assignments, tests, and sports activities in the face of DPN.

Teddy and Howie did not envy the faculty right now. They had a tremendous job ahead of them. It would take real courage to stand up against the vaunted board and tell them of their support of DPN. It might or might not happen, but at least there were many professors who would stand with them. It might cost them their jobs, but with the number of faculty joining them along with students and other staff members, Teddy doubted that they would be fired.

It was time for dinner this Monday early evening, and they had earned a good meal in the cafeteria. Teddy was recognized by students as he walked down the campus road. Passing the Bison, Teddy smiled as he thought about the Sunday night bonfire that students had made by lighting up the pile of press releases. Imagine, the board had been too frightened to come to the campus, so they hired one single guy in a

VW to drop off the copies and slink off like a dog with its tail between its legs. They just had no class at all. Cowards! There was Ely Center, where Howie and he spent so much time in the Rat eating pizza and drinking Coke after classes.

Ah, the football field with the bleachers. That was where the pre-DPN rally had been held the previous Tuesday, which saw Teddy come out of his shell as a "D"eaf person for the first time in his life, and led to his active involvement in DPN starting Sunday night. Teddy remembered that Tuesday morning like it had just happened today.

He heard about the rally from his classmates and somehow he ended up having a copy of a blue bumper sticker that said "DEAF PRESIDENT NOW" on it. He had decided to wear it on his forehead and also make a billboard from cardboard paper which he found in the Education Department supplies room. On the front, he wrote a slogan: "It is time for a Deaf President … NOW!" On the back poster board, he wrote: "The board must not pick a hearing president AGAIN!" He had tied the two poster boards with yarn and after breakfast, he put it on with the bumper sticker on his forehead. Trudging over to the football field, someone had motioned to him and asked him to stand at the silver fence right in front of the bleachers.

Soon enough, the bleachers were full of students. There were other students standing near Teddy, all with different placards. One made him laugh the most, something about Zinser. He could not remember what it had said, but it made him laugh when he saw it. So many speakers had come to inspire the crowd, including leaders from the National Association of the Deaf, Student Body Government, and other organizations. Everyone was fired up and nobody believed that the board would be stupid enough to pick Zinser, except for Luis and a few others who feared the worst.

The rally had gone on for approximately two hours; then everyone dispersed. The following morning, people had said to Teddy, "Way to go! You are famous!" Teddy had no idea what they were talking about until someone showed him the front page of *The Washington Post* metro section. There he was, standing there with that bumper sticker on his forehead. What a great photo that was! Big also -- 5x7. He had bought several copies of the Post that morning, and he wrote to his family the first chance he got. What an exciting day it was. Even his oldest friend Carla's mother had written to him from Long Island.

Funny about Carla. She should be there, as she had graduated from Gallaudet with a degree in biology. Her dad had been like Teddy's second father his whole life. While Gary had not signed for him or Carla, he had always taken the time to talk to them eye-to-eye. One time, Teddy had an asthma attack in Carla's basement during a party. Gary was a doctor and injected Teddy with some medication that relieved his asthmatic symptoms. It was either that or a sure trip to the ER, so he never forgot what Gary did for him. That was why it was such a blow when Gary passed away in 1983 from leukemia. He even remembered when he and Carla flew home from RIT, the very moment when Carla was told about her father's death. He shuddered at the memory.

Carla had been his first "girlfriend," and he had told Gary that he would marry her when he grew up. Gary and the other adults who heard him say that chuckled, and Gary bounced him on his lap like his own son. Teddy wished that Gary had lived to see this protest happen. Maybe he was watching from above. That would be nice, if he could know for sure. He silently said a prayer for Gary and Carla.

There was Benson Hall. Only freshmen lived there this year for whatever reason, and it was a pigsty! Teddy was glad he did not have to endure that and quickly walked past it up the circling ramp to the open space that led to Cogswell and Krug. As he lived in Cogswell, that was where he had the most memories. He remembered the first day he walked into the first-floor area where the lobby was. He had looked around and noticed that the stairs had a silver metal plate attached to the sidebar.

He asked around as to why Cogswell had one, and not Krug. Then he found out that in the past, Cogswell had been a women's dorm so whenever a guy would come in, he had to wait for the housemaster to go "fetch" the girl from her room. After a while, guys figured out that if they stood in a certain area on the first floor, they could look up at the ceiling and see a girl's skirt as she walked down the stairs with the housemistress. Once the administration found out about this, then the steel bar was put in place on the rails, so guys could not look up a girl's skirt anymore. This was one of Gallaudet's best-kept secrets, and he never tired of making other students and visitors laugh with this nugget of information.

Should he go straight to his room, or forget that and grab dinner with his friends Michael and Sharona? Funny how that couple had met in the same orientation with Teddy. At first, Sharona was attracted to Teddy, but one day at dinner, Mike put some food in Teddy's milk while he was looking away at someone else.

When Teddy's attention came back to the table, he lost his temper and threw the glass of milk at another student who tended to play pranks on him. Then, when Mike confessed it was him, Teddy had stormed off in a huff. That was when Sharona decided to date Mike, not Teddy. He wished he had kept his cool and laughed. That would have clinched Sharona dating him, rather than Mike. But they remained good friends and often went out on the town, the three of them.

Once he entered the cafeteria, he immediately noticed Mike and Sharona at their usual table. After getting his food and milk on a tray, he ambled over and sat down at their table in his regular chair. It was funny, like *Cheers,* when Norm Peterson would enter the bar and everyone yelled "Norm!" It was a place where everyone knew your name, and people could sit in their usual spot without worrying that someone else would take it from you.

"Hey, Mike. What's going on? Why is everyone bustling and making a big deal?" Teddy could see that students were not eating much, as they were deep in conversation around him.

"The news just got out about Alumni House, which is now the center of activity for the deaf protest leaders. Greg, Jerry, Tim, and Bridgetta are closeted up there 24/7 with faculty, interpreters, and outside advisors trying to maintain the status quo and keeping up the momentum that we have had since Sunday night. The gates have been opened, but nobody is going to class and the faculty is meeting today to decide whether to support the protest. If they do, then Spilman and the board members are cooked!"

Teddy took the news with glee. This was a good development, and it was only twenty-four hours since the protest had begun. He could only imagine how Zinser was feeling. He heard she was a very nice person, but the board had not been fair to her. She had no idea what she was getting into by being chosen. She did not understand that deaf culture was so intertwined with Gallaudet, going back to 1864 when it was founded by Edward Miner Gallaudet with the signature of President Abraham Lincoln. But the roots of Gallaudet went back much further than that.

Before 1817, there had been little in way of instruction for deaf people in America. One summer day, a seminary student named Thomas Hopkins Gallaudet sat on the porch of his parents' home in Connecticut, as he was on vacation from school. He was sick often, so he was recuperating at the time. He immediately noticed a young girl sitting on the ground all by herself with a stick in her hand. There were kids her age playing nearby. He wondered why they were not including her in their play. Gallaudet got up and looked for someone to ask. He found out that this girl was deaf, and her name was Alice Cogswell.

He recognized the last name. Her father was Mason Cogswell, who was a wealthy and well-known man locally. Her mother was Mary Cogswell. Ironic, wasn't it? A man of money, and there was nothing he had done to help his daughter. How could he, a young seminarian who had never met a deaf person, communicate with her and see if she had any potential? After all, she was a child of God and deserved the same opportunity to read the Bible and understand the grace of Jesus Christ's salvation. Thus she could enter heaven like any hearing person.

He walked over to Alice tentatively and tapped her on the right shoulder. Alice's body jerked forward and her face craned upward to see who had called for her attention. Gallaudet smiled nervously down at her and he crouched so their eyes were level. Such a pretty and innocent girl. She was so alone and her eyes looked sad. He glanced over at the boys and girls who had been playing. Maybe one day she would be included. Now to see if she had any intelligence. What word should he start off with? Aha, "hat."

Was there another stick on the ground nearby? Yes, there was! He grabbed it and wrote H-A-T on the dirt ground. Then, he took his hat off and pointed at it. His eyes darted from the black top hat to Alice and back to the top hat. Then, he tapped his forehead twice with his right hand and with the stick in his left hand, he pointed to H-A-T. Would she understand this? To his amazement, the girl smiled broadly and pointed at the word with her left index finger and then tapped her forehead twice. She did understand! She screamed with delight and laughed out loud.

Her father came running outside of the house and exclaimed, "What happened here? Why is my daughter screaming and laughing? Such an unusual sound, coming from Alice. Who are you?"

Gallaudet cleared his throat and stood up to his full posture. This was a very important man, so he had to be at his best now. "I am Thomas Hopkins Gallaudet, sir. I just communicated the word H-A-T with Alice, your daughter. She does understand language and concepts. We must help her learn to read and write!"

Cogswell gaped at his daughter and noticed a happy expression on her face. He had never seen her like this. Yes! They must do something for Alice to enrich her life, to introduce her to society like a proper woman.

"Mr. Gallaudet, do you think you can find out if there is schooling anywhere in England for our daughter? We will gladly pay for your ship fare over there. Please?" Cogswell's face was almost pleading. He surely wanted his daughter to be educated.

"Yes, I would do that. When you have the funds ready, I will go to England and find out what's there for deaf students."

Cogswell's face softened and he grasped Gallaudet's hand, shaking it hard for several seconds. "Wonderful! I am a man of means, so ship fare will not be a problem. When can you depart from Boston Harbor? I am ready to pay your fare."

Hmmm, Gallaudet thought. *The sooner the better*. He had plenty of time on his hands, as he had tried different occupations and none of them suited him. He had tried law, clerking, peddling as a salesman, and studying in the ministry. None of them seemed right to him and with his frail health, he did not feel any of those jobs suited him. Why not go to England, and see a little bit of the world at the same time on someone else's dime?

"I can depart as soon as possible, Mr. Cogswell. Let's get this started!" Gallaudet wrote down his full name and age so Cogswell could buy his ticket at the station. Eventually, Gallaudet wound up at the oral school in England, but when he was told he had to pay for the services of the Braidwood family who ran the school with the oral method, he declined. As fortune would have it, he saw a flyer for a lecture by a French educator of the deaf, Abbee Sicard, and his star deaf pupil, Laurent Clerc. One thing led to another and Gallaudet ended up in France learning from Sicard and Clerc in sign language.

Gallaudet convinced Clerc to come to America with him by boat. So, Clerc was known as the father of deaf education in America, just like George Washington was known as the "father of our country."

Teddy very much doubted Zinser could have told that story, or have identified the statue of the girl, Alice Cogswell, with Thomas Hopkins Gallaudet. This statue overlooked the campus and everyone had looked at this statue with pride over the years, especially on Sunday and Monday. In fact, he wondered how many administrators and board members knew who the two individuals were. Without Gallaudet, Clerc, and Alice, there would have been no deaf education. It truly was amazing how one small incident had such enormous ripples throughout history.

Chapter Three:

Tuesday, March 8th, 1988

uesday passed with little incident except for rallies and meetings.
Teddy spent the entire day talking to everyone, attending the rallies in various places, and brainstorming sessions to discuss "what if"
the protest lasted through spring break. Plans were drawn on how
students could appeal to airlines, hotels, cruises, and other places to
get a refund due to the board's refusal to give in to the four demands.
It was unreal to Teddy that he could walk past his classrooms in Fowler
Hall where he usually attended graduate classes and seminars for education students.

Many students did not know Fowler Hall at all, even though
they were inside that building regularly for classes like he was. It was
originally a women's residence dormitory built in 1918, named after
Sophia Fowler Gallaudet, who was the wife of Thomas H. Gallaudet.
She was one of the first students at the American School for the Deaf in
Hartford, Connecticut, when Laurent Clerc founded it. She had met
Gallaudet after graduating from ASD. They had eight children, including Edward Miner Gallaudet. Teddy's classes were usually on the third
floor, except for his computer class which was on the fourth floor.

Usually, Fowler Hall was bustling with activity, but it was closed
shut today because of the number of people mingling in front of that
building. Campus security had people walking around to make sure
that there was no violence. Amazingly, from Sunday night to Tuesday
night, there had been no incidents of violence. The DC police found
that remarkable. Students knew that any violence would damage the
protest's validity, so leaders were emphatic at rallies and meetings to
tell students not to provoke anyone to anger.

One important event did happen on this Tuesday, a day with glorious weather and nary a cloud in the sky. The American flag proudly flew over Chapel Hall as a horde of students, faculty, and other people walked around holding signs. His favorite one was "Overcome the Day of Infamy," an obvious referent to Pearl Harbor when the Japanese launched a surprise attack on December 7th, 1941. The Gallaudet University Alumni Association voted to support the students and their four demands, plus they donated $1,000 to the Deaf President Now fund, which was accepting contributions from anyone and everyone.

As Teddy walked by Chapel Hall, he could see a group of deaf kids arguing with some adults. He was by nature a very curious person, so he stopped in his tracks. What was this? Looked serious. He walked over to one of the boys who looked like he was around fifteen years of age.

"Hi, is there a problem? Can I help you out here?" Teddy glanced at the adults, who were visibly upset. There was a mixture of men and women standing a few feet away. One woman was crying and others were trying to comfort her.

"Those are our parents. My name is Ben. I am a student at MSSD and my folks want me to go home. I refuse to because this protest is mine as much as it is for the college students! I want to be involved in this historic moment. It is our fight. Age does not matter!"

Ben had tears in his eyes as he signed how he felt. Wow. What a strong attitude for a teenager, Teddy felt. Ben was very brave to defy his parents' wishes. Was he right or wrong? That was not for Teddy to decide.

"Excuse me. Are you Ben's parents? My name is Teddy and I am a graduate student at Gallaudet. Why do you want Ben to go home?"

The parents should know better, in Teddy's mind. MSSD was the Model Secondary School for the Deaf, which was founded in 1966 by President Lyndon Johnson with PL 89-694. Its doors first opened in 1969 after the federal government authorized its operation on the

Gallaudet campus. Students went to MSSD for free from any state and territory. Of course, students would feel strongly that their involvement in this protest was warranted. Now he had to convince the group of parents.

"Before you answer my question," said Teddy, "please let me tell you something. I can see that your son is very intelligent and feels strongly about this movement. If you saw something that you really felt was wrong, wouldn't you speak up about it? For instance, these students may become Gallaudet's future. Do they want a president who cannot sign one single word? Heck, no! You should be proud of Ben!"

Teddy looked around him at the other parents who were standing there. The kids' faces showed pride and strength that became more evident as he talked to the parents. Luckily, he could speak very well and sign at the same time. It was not the ideal mode of communication, but it would have to do. He was very thankful to his parents for having enabled him to speak so fluently growing up. His mom quit her teaching job to stay home with him and teach him, using the John Tracy Clinic correspondence course.

The parents' faces softened, and one by one they told their kids to stay for the protest. But they would have to behave themselves in the dorms on the school campus, which was at the eastern end of the university-wide campus, on top of a hill overlooking Kendall Green. It was all brick buildings, and many of the students resided there full time instead of commuting back and forth like many deaf students did at other schools.

Chapter Four:

Wednesday, March 9th, 1988

O n Wednesday morning, Teddy was in the cafeteria for breakfast. He always had the same thing every morning: oatmeal, chocolate milk, buttered toast, and orange juice. He liked routine and did not like change unless he absolutely had to divert from his usual daily regimen. That meant Teddy could not work at a freelance job where he would have to travel from one place to another. Being a teacher would enable him to adhere to the same scheduled blocks every day in the same classroom.

He saw Howie sitting at his usual table and he sauntered over to him, carrying his tray. Howie was animatedly talking to a few people that Teddy did not recognize. What was going on? Howie did not excite easily, so that meant this was going to be good.

"What's going on, Howie?" Teddy looked at all the people at the table. They stopped signing and one of them gestured to Howie to tell him the news.

"Mornin', Teddy! There are some exciting developments that will happen today. For one, there is gonna be a meeting soon between student leaders and some faculty members and a couple of congressmen, David Bonior of Michigan and Steve Gunderson of Wisconsin. Did you know that Jack Gannon, the director of the alumni association, was contacted by Bonior to set up this meeting? Greg Hlibok is also going to be at this pow-wow today!"

Teddy thought for a minute. Congressmen on the board? Of course! He had forgotten that two congressmen and a senator were appointed to serve on the university board. How could he have forgotten that? Where was Senator Daniel Inouye of Hawaii?

"Howie, is Senator Inouye gonna be at the meeting also? I thought he was on the board as well?"

Teddy looked askance at all the students at the table and a few of them shrugged. Obviously, they were as clueless as he was. They would find out eventually through the grapevine. Teddy chuckled at the thought. Hearing people's gossip had nothing on deaf culture gossip. It was like a raging forest fire, as the deaf world was much smaller and more condensed than the hearing world. There were six degrees of separation in mainstream society, but only two degrees in the deaf society. Or so the saying went.

Where was Zinser right now, anyway? Teddy was curious if she had yet arrived in Washington, DC to assume her duties as the next president of Gallaudet. Unbeknownst to Teddy and many other students, Zinser did arrive very early in the morning to start working visibly so that her presence could help bring the protest to a close quickly. Teddy and most of the other students would laugh at this, because there was just no way they would give in this soon.

Teddy sat at his table in the cafeteria with Howie. All of a sudden, there was a flurry of activity and one of the students jumped on the platform to make an announcement. Now this should be good! All faces turned to this student with expectation and they were not disappointed.

"Guess what, people? Zinser just thumbed her nose at the protest. She actually said, 'I am in charge!' thus destroying any chance of mediation. Did you know that Peabody Fitzpatrick is the PR firm handling this for the board? They are well-known in the DC circles, so we gotta fight back harder!"

Teddy gaped and so did everyone else. How could Zinser be so arrogant as to make such a statement? First, Spilman with her "Deaf people are not ready to function in a hearing world," and now Zinser's "I am in charge!" These people were just clueless. Beyond clueless! Teddy would never understand it in a million years.

"Also...your attention please!" The student on the platform banged the floor with his shoes. "There will be an announcement at noon with King Jordan and Zinser! Be there!" He stepped off the platform and as students pestered him with questions, he shrugged his shoulders. He obviously did not know much, just like everyone else.

Teddy was perturbed. He did not have a good feeling about the upcoming noon press conference. His Spidey sixth sense was tingling again. King Jordan was not going to publicly support their protest. No way. Not with Spilman and Zinser breathing down his neck!

"Hey, Howie! Let's make sure we watch the press conference either in person or on TV. Wanna do that?"

Howie's head was hanging. His chin touched his chest and he was obviously very upset. "Teddy, I think Jordan is going to turn traitor on us and run!"

"I agree with you, buddy. But I wanna see this for myself, not hear it from someone else! I just hope we both are wrong!"

They walked from the cafeteria past the dorms, deep in thought. Although they did not say a word to each other, each of them knew what the other was thinking and feeling. Betrayal. How could King Jordan possibly support the board of trustees in the selection of Zinser? That would be a dagger in everyone's heart, especially with so many faculty and GUAA supporting the ouster of Zinser.

The wind blew in their faces as if a signal of struggle was ahead. They had to strain to walk against the breeze.

"Howie, I hope this is not an omen. Suddenly, it is getting more difficult to walk across campus against this strong wind. I just hope we are not setting ourselves up for another betrayal by someone who does not understand the Deaf world!"

Teddy had a worried look on his face and his eyes moistened over. He had had enough of disappointment. Just recently, he had been extremely distraught when his family was on a trip to Florida for a week over December vacation. The last night he was there, his family played a Pictionary game and Rosemary had a card that said the word "SON" so she drew a picture of a sun. Of course, her partner Kathleen, his younger sister, said the wrong word but the right sound.

So, he had asked her to spell it and she said S-U-N which should have invalidated the point. But his parents gave it to her, and he lost it right there and then. That was the straw that broke the camel's back. He paced all over the living room of his Uncle Benny's house in Orlando. Finally, he said, "Mom, Dad, I am going back to New York tomorrow morning instead of later this week. I will drive to Gallaudet in a few days! I am going to pack my bags now."

His parents had been shocked but accepted his decision. Of course, his sisters were more than happy to have him out of their hair sooner. The next day, he boarded a plane headed for Islip and in a few days, he followed his good friend Bella to Gallaudet, where he started his new chapter as a student at the only liberal arts university solely for the deaf in the world.

Now this was going to be even worse, Jordan announcing his backing of Zinser, if the rumors were actually true. In fact, Teddy was not that surprised that Jordan would do this, as he was scared for his administrative job as the dean of the College of Arts and Sciences, but he still did not understand why Jordan could not have enough spunk and courage to stand his ground like so many others had before him. Look at Rosa Parks, a mild-mannered African-American woman who was minding her own business when a white person ordered her to move to the back of the bus. She had refused and was arrested and, put in jail, which ignited the civil rights movement and Martin Luther King, Jr.'s ascendance to prominence.

Passing the library on the right, Teddy and Howie just kept walking. They could see students inside, seated at tables near the windows, signing at a frenzied pace. The only topic today was Jordan's expected support of Zinser. In fact, everyone had a new moniker for her: Sinner! That became her sign name as the week progressed and it was already common knowledge, especially with her pronouncement that morning that she was officially in charge.

Teddy had a special place in his heart for the library. He had grown up in his hometown frequenting the library, riding on his bike at least twice a week, relishing the chance to read more and more books. Everyone knew him there and when he walked in, people would yell, "Hey, Teddy! How are you? How many books is that this month?" He took the ribbing good-naturedly. Once he had even seen his high school crush, Jenny, there with a study group, and he had frozen in his tracks. He chuckled at the memory. Seemed so long ago this week, with everything that was happening.

"Teddy, hey! Snap out of it!" Howie mock-tackled him and made sure he did it gently. After all, he was a much bigger and stronger guy than Teddy, and he didn't want to see him hurt for no reason. "Look! There are so many people here!"

Teddy's eyes roamed around the back of Chapel Hall. They were not even near the front side, and yet there were so many people milling about. There were facial expressions of anger, tension, and sadness. So the rumors were probably true! It was a difference between the hearing and deaf worlds with gossip. Anything that happened in the deaf world quickly spread around in different circles.

That reminded him of something that had happened during his RIT-Christian days. His best friend, Pete, who had moved to California when they were both in second grade, had heard about his conversion to the born-again Christian lifestyle and wrote him a letter about it. Teddy had been surprised, and this introduced him to the "two degrees of separation" of the deaf world as compared to the "six degrees" in the hearing world.

He wished Pete was here. What a guy that was. He reminded Teddy of John Cusack in *The Sure Thing* with Anthony Edwards as a party go-to guy in Palm Springs, California and Cusack as this miserable Northeastener going to college in a frigid winter. Somehow, Edwards told Cusack about this "sure thing" girl who was waiting for him over Christmas break, so he had to join a ride out there across the country to meet her. It was one of Teddy's favorite movies and never failed to make him laugh.

Pete was the homecoming king of his college, even though there were only 150 deaf students and 30,000 hearing students. It was a reflection of Pete's personality and swimming ability, winning medals in college meets at the Division II level. When Pete and his family moved to California, it had been like a dagger in Teddy's heart. A few months after the move, Teddy had leafed through his mom's phone book and proceeded to dial Pete's home phone number even though he couldn't hear anything on the other end.

Not sure if anyone had picked up the phone in Pete's apartment, he kept saying, "Hello? Hello? This is Teddy. Is Pete there?" After a few seconds, his mom came downstairs and saw Teddy talking into the phone mouthpiece. She had grabbed the phone and hung it up, then her face turned to him.

"What were you doing on the phone, Teddy?" She was puzzled because he was unable to hear what was said on the other end, even with the Oticon hearing aids that he wore.

"I wanted to talk to Pete! I miss him!" He was very upset and broke down crying. It was so lonely here being surrounded by a family that talked amongst themselves as if he was not even there.

As they got older, they had kept in touch via letters and postcards. He went to visit California to visit Pete's family when he was in fifth grade. That flight from JFK had been the toughest ride of his life, as he remembered embarking on the huge 747 holding the hand of the stewardess who towered above his head. He was on the verge of tears and felt utterly alone, never having been away from his parents like this. But the stewardess had done a good job of making him feel at home. He got a flight pin and she kept him busy with books, plus she sat down next to him occasionally during the flight.

When he got to California and saw Pete with his family, he was better. Every morning, Pete was not in his bed. He later found out Pete was at swimming practice at 5 a.m., like clockwork. That had really impressed Teddy to a huge extent. Pete was dedicated. That whole week had zipped by like it was a few seconds. Then Pete flew out to visit Teddy in Long Island during sixth grade. Maureen had really liked him, which bothered Teddy, but he couldn't do anything about it.

The best memory he had of Pete was their families' trip to Baja, Mexico when they were thirteen. Teddy had gotten really sick from a restaurant they stopped at for lunch. He had not heeded warnings about the dirty water – plus, who knew how clean or dirty the restaurant's kitchen was! When they got to the hotel, Teddy had run to the bathroom and in a few minutes, the toilet water was overflowing.

Pete's younger brother, Donny, was sitting on his bed reading a book. When he saw that the hotel room was flooded with one inch's worth of water from the toilet, he started screaming. Teddy's dad had come in, walking through the water in his expensive shoes, and carried Donny out.

In a split second, they all decided to grab their stuff and get out, because the water was seeping into the hallway already. They sped back to the Mexican side of the border and once they got back to San Diego, Teddy and Pete got out of the van at the first shopping center they got to. They were on their knees, kissing the ground thankful to be out of Mexico.

Teddy smiled at the memories of Pete. He had missed Pete all those years -- and then he realized that Pete definitely had heard about this protest. Hopefully, they would touch base soon. Suddenly, people started walking away from Chapel Hall. Teddy and Howie were puzzled at this and started asking around what had happened.

The gist of it was that Jordan just made his announcement as expected, backing Zinser. Boos and hisses spread through the crowd watching, and there were news cameras catching the whole thing. Teddy glanced over at a group of students standing near the entrance to Fowler Hall. Their faces looked ashen as their eyes stared steadfastly at the ground below them. It was like night and day, as he remembered them from the past few days on campus, supporting the protest.

Many of them were even dressed like they were going to a funeral. They had all-black attire, and gray or black overcoats, due to the chilliness in the air that day (both literally and figuratively), and the women had no makeup on. Teddy wondered what the significance of that was. Their hands were in pockets and they walked very slowly away from Carlin. One or two were crying, and everyone could see it. There was no effort to wipe the tears away as they dropped to the sidewalk, leaving a trail of wet splotches.

It reminded Teddy of the preparatory students' rat funeral that they held every year to signify the end of their prep year and entrance into the freshman class of the following September. This was one of the major events of the school calendar and he had seen pictures of the procession. This group of students right now did look like such a somber crowd, and he realized that this was just as bad as a funeral, because it was the "death" of their adoration of King Jordan, who had been a psychology professor for years before moving into administration. So many students had raved about Jordan as a teacher, role model, and campus figure that this announcement just had to pierce their hearts.

"Howie, is Zinser on campus now?" Howie glanced at Teddy and shrugged. He really did not care if Zinser was anywhere on campus or nearby. He was devastated. Growing up at Staunton, he had seen too many hearing administrators run the school with mediocre sign skills, or even none. But that did not lessen his pain at seeing Jordan jump ship and abandon the DPN movement.

Teddy was really curious if she had the bravado of that hearing board member who had tried to enter campus through the MSSD entrance earlier that week. He continued to look around and look for familiar faces. Luis! There he was! Trudging slowly past him, not even seeing him. *How unlike Luis*, Teddy mused. Luis was always lively and bouncing around, saying hello to everyone, being his usual personable self.

But not today. His chin almost touched his chest, and his hands were buried in his pockets. Teddy would never have recognized him if he did not see him every day. He had not even shaved, and had a New Orleans Saints hat on, lowered to cover half of his face. Luis was from Louisiana, so that was why he had such loyalty to a terrible football team like that.

Teddy wondered how Rhonda was faring in her dorm room, hiding from everyone on campus. Ever since he told Howie and a few others about her pro-Zinser stance, she had not been visible. She had even called for delivery of pizza and Chinese food so she would not have to make herself appear in public. People looked at her with daggers in their eyes.

He felt bad for her in a way, but felt vindicated in another way. He wanted to go check on her in spite of how he felt about her support for the board's selection. Yes, he really should! He cared about this girl no matter what. His anger and resentment had faded somewhat. He was ready to see her. Even just to talk about the weather, nothing else.

"Howie, are you up to a trek to Rhonda's room? I am worried about her and want to see how she is doing. Are you with me?" Teddy looked at Howie, hoping he would go with him in spite of his feelings about her not being a good match for Teddy.

"Teddy! You actually want to see Rhonda after everything that has happened since Sunday? Man, what am I going to do with you?" Howie shook his head and then sighed. He put his left arm around Teddy's neck and pretended to do a Hulk Hogan move, which was to do an armlock of the opponent's neck, then mash his forehead. Teddy laughed and felt relieved Howie would go with him.

It was a surreal walk across campus, seeing everyone so passive and stunned. This morning, there had been so much signing around them, and now it was visually quiet. Students who were signing frantically just an hour ago were sitting at their tables in the library on the second floor, heads buried in their hands. Nobody needed to say or sign anything. Everyone felt the same way right now, a shared emotion of disappointment and shock.

Finally, Clerc Hall. Teddy quickened his step and Howie hurried to keep up with him. It was better to get this over with. See how Rhonda was and quickly leave before anyone saw them there. It was like the kiss of death to be seen with her. They entered the lobby and waited for the elevator. When they got to the third floor, Teddy pivoted on his right foot and headed to her door.

Nobody had seen them yet, which would have been highly unlikely any other day of their time here at Gallaudet, but this day was never going to happen again, God willing! Teddy stepped to the door, took a deep breath, and rang the bell. No sound came out, as this was a visually-oriented campus. Teddy knew that all the dorm rooms had a strobe light that went on and off whenever someone rang the bell.

Bracing himself for the moment the door opened and he saw her face, Teddy steeled himself not to let his heart melt. He had been hopelessly in love with her just the other day until the "conversation" happened. But he still cared about this woman and was concerned about her welfare. No answer? What was that on her door? A note to him? Why hadn't he noticed it before? The envelope said "MOORE" which was a secret name that Rhonda had given Teddy. Moore was Ted Kennedy's middle name and nobody would have put two and two together.

"Howie, look at this!" Teddy snatched the envelope that was taped on Rhonda's door and they quickly walked away to the TV lounge, where there were a couple of sofas. Nobody was there. Howie stared at Teddy with an disbelieving look on his face. A note? MOORE? What was that all about? He looked at Teddy questioningly and gestured to the envelope.

"Teddy, man, what is MOORE?"

"Oh, that is Rhonda's secret name for me. Remember Edward Kennedy's middle name? That way, in an emergency, I would know it was her and only her who wrote the note to me. Nobody can forge a letter and fool me this way. My name for her is Joan, which is a joke because that's his ex-wife."

Howie "Ahhh'ed" and nodded his head. That was good sense. It was too easy to write a note and copy someone else's handwriting. Let's see what Rhonda had to say! He wondered how Teddy was feeling right now. It couldn't be easy for his best friend to go to this girl's room and then find an envelope addressed to him.

"Is it OK if I read it with you, or do you want to read it first alone?" Howie always wanted to respect Teddy's privacy, especially at a sensitive time like this.

"Thanks, Howie. I want to skim it over first -- then we can read it together. Let's see..." Teddy slowly opened the envelope, ripping apart the back and tenderly taking out the paper inside. His eyes widened as he started to read...

My dearest Teddy Moore,

If you are reading this, I am relieved because you will know where I am. As of Tuesday morning. I am on my way off campus to go back to Long Island. I needed some time away from Gallaudet and you. This whole protest has really shown me that I am not yet ready for a full immersion in the Deaf world. You were very emphatic in your disagreement with my support of Zinser. I need to go home, be with my parents in Queens. You know where to find me. I am waiting for all of this to blow over and then maybe I will come back.

All classes have been canceled anyway, so I am grabbing this opportunity to drive home and spend time by myself, be with my family and hearing friends, rethink why I stood against the protest, and enjoy my family dog. I really need this. I wanted to thank you for a wonderful two months together as friends. Just an FYI: I broke up with my boyfriend at Catholic University. He was a nice guy, always respected me. But I realized after meeting you that he was not the guy I wanted. You are!

Teddy looked up from the sheet and his eyes moistened. "Howie, she broke up with Roy, her boyfriend at Catholic!"

Howie gasped. "NO way! She actually did? What else did she say?"

"Scoot on over, read it with me. I don't want to keep you in suspense any longer. Come on!" Both sets of eyes went back to the letter and they started reading again.

You always make me feel safe. Loved. Wanted. Cherished. That is what I need in a man for the future. Plus I love ASL and the Deaf world. You are an integral part of it. I want to be with you. Spend days and nights next to you. But please let me have this time by myself before I come back and be with you.

You always make me laugh. I have been abused by men before, including my uncle, who was always leering at me. I know I am very pretty, but I never felt this way until I met you. The times we spent at Union Station eating dinner, playing around with food, making up stories about people walking near us, signing with our mouths full, eyes taking in each other's presence.

I wish I had told you before how I felt, but now I am doing it. Taking the plunge. Will you be mine? I want to be all yours. I love you. I have always loved you, Teddy. I want you to show me everything in your life. Your hometown. Your family. I want to interpret for you at gatherings, parties. It will not be easy, but I want to do it more than anything. I want to share the deaf world with you. I will never feel as safe as I do with you. If you want to get in touch with me, you know my home mailing address in New Hyde Park. You are my favorite PITA!

Love with xoxo,
Rhonda

Teddy whistled and took a long, deep breath. Wow! That was quite a letter. He was so happy that Rhonda felt the same way he did about her. Wasn't everyone entitled to his or her own opinion about the protest? Yes, she did hurt him by disagreeing with students' demands in opposition to Zinser, but it took strength for her to take this stand. He had been too blind to see that the other day. But she seemed to admit she had made a mistake and she wanted to join the protest sentiment. This was good news. He had finally found the love of his life.

"Teddy, I stand corrected…she really loves you and she supports the protest also. You could spend the rest of your lifetime looking for another woman like this and never find her! Remember your Uncle Benny? That story you told me about him."

Teddy knew what Howie was talking about. When Uncle Benny was young, in his twenties, he had fallen in love with a beautiful, vibrant, popular girl named Beatrice. Everyone called her Bee, as she was always hosting parties for anything and she was like a queen bee, delegating responsibilities and errands to everyone else, keeping the party organized and running on schedule. She had reminded everyone of Aunt Bee on *The Andy Griffith Show* from the '50s. Similar personality, but an updated version in terms of clothes and accessories.

In any case, Bee's parents had been opposed to her marrying Benny just because he was Catholic and she was not. It seemed that Benny was not "good enough" for them, as he was not athletic, ruggedly handsome, and trendy. He wore terrible clothes and drove a beat-up Ford. Bee did not care about any of that, but her parents did. Even though Benny was really smart and had been accepted to Yale, her parents did not want her to be with him. They had even threatened her with being disowned from their wealth if she married him. So, to make a long story short, she broke up with him and married some guy who was the son of her parents' closest friends.

This had broken Benny's heart. He never went out with another girl seriously after that. He dove into his legal career and joined his father's law firm, making it Cooperman, Cooperman, Esq. His father had been pleased to have his son working with him side by side, but he hated to see Benny broken-hearted day after day, year after year.

He had tried to set Benny up with daughters of his friends, but to no avail.

Approximately six or seven years later, Bee told Benny that she was divorced and her parents had passed away. Plus, she had two daughters aged five and three. Benny had turned down her plea for a second chance together with nobody to stop them. So, Bee walked away very sad and never remarried. She still loved Benny with all her heart.

Teddy was relieved that he did not end up like Benny after reading Rhonda's note. He easily could have, after his stubborn streak manifested itself when he argued with her the other day. He counted his blessings to have met a girl like Rhonda who accepted him as a deaf person using ASL. Plus, she was on her way to becoming fluent also.

There was Mimi to think about also. But she had a boyfriend, Randy, so that was out of the question for him to even consider. He refused to put his dating life on hold for any girl in his life. If you had asked him in high school what kind of girl he would end up with, he definitely would have picked Mimi. She was a really fashionable dresser, knew how to carry herself, was popular with everyone. Rhonda dressed more simply for convenience, although she did look nice. But nothing like Mimi, whose family had a lot of money and a really big ranch house in Bethesda, Maryland.

He wondered how Rhonda was doing at home on Long Island right now. He would have to give her some time to herself before she came back to him. It was like the old adage on his favorite poster in high school: "If you love someone, let her go. If she comes back, she is yours. If she doesn't, she never was."

Love was not something you could force on someone. If you tried to convince a person to love you, that was more like abuse, with controlling behaviors and oppression. That never resulted in true happiness. He had seen some couples like that on campus and he never wanted something even close to such a negative vibe. Rhonda…Rhonda…he missed her.

Rhonda Jennings lay back on her bed at her parents' house. What a week it had been, not even! Just a couple of days ago, she had been steamrolled (or it seemed like) by a good friend of hers, Teddy, because of her support for Zinser. That had backfired on her in such a big way that it really surprised her. Thank God she was safe at home in New Hyde Park.

She had actually feared for her safety on the Gallaudet campus, surrounded by students who could not fathom how she was opposed to the protest and their four demands. She would never forget the long drive from Gallaudet to New York that Tuesday morning, March 8th, leaving early to avoid detection on campus as she walked quickly to her car from Clerc Hall.

Luckily, nobody had seen her at 6:00 a.m., as she raced down the stairs to the parking lot below the dorm. It was still dark out as she threw a laundry bag in the trunk. She figured she would wash her clothes when she got to her parents', thus having enough clothes to tide her over for a while. Nobody was ever here this early so she felt safe getting out of her room. She missed Teddy already. He was the only guy she had really felt good with, and she might just have blown that.

The letter. Hopefully, he would come by her room after a day or two of cooling off. She had written "MOORE" on the envelope so that he would recognize it when he saw it, her secret name for him. How funny that was — nobody would ever guess who MOORE was. Not even Howie, who detested her and wanted Teddy to have nothing more to do with her. She thought about him all the time. Just last night, she had snuck out late to Catholic University to meet her boyfriend, Roy. She felt different with him after having met Teddy. It was hard to place it. It had been a rough evening breaking up with Roy, and she remembered the entire conversation as it had happened.

She had seen how casual Roy was to see her, not bringing her any flowers, never treating her to a spa day, that girly stuff she needed.

Teddy already had bought her some nice yellow roses the other week just to celebrate their special friendship. She liked that kind of man, who showed her how worthy she was, and she craved the attention that Teddy gave her without a second thought. Roy had been so opposite of Teddy. It really floored her to think that she had accepted the status quo prior to meeting Teddy.

She knew she had to eventually get out of bed and start on her day. Facing her parents was not going to be easy, as she wanted to tell them about her realization about Teddy, her feelings, the DPN movement, everything. They were more old-fashioned, not showing her much affection. They had not really communicated with her as she grew up on Long Island. This had led her to expect a boyfriend to be the same way, but she was quickly finding out what it really was that made her happy.

Her mouth was suddenly dry. Water. She threw back her covers and landed her two feet on the wooden floor. Good thing it was not too cold outside. When winter came, the floor was unbearably cold and she would have worn socks when sleeping. But it was much warmer today, so she was relieved.

Let's get this show on the road, Rhonda! She wiped her eyes, which were red from crying the past few days. There were absolutely no tears left inside her. She wondered how long it would take for her body to make new tears. It had been like a faucet turned all the way on as she drove home and slept fitfully through the night.

She had her own bathroom, which she really appreciated as a perk. Many of her friends had to wait for someone else to finish up in there whether it was a shower or a call from mother nature. The countertop was all silver marble and her feet slid along the tiled black floor. Ugh, the reflection in the mirror showed her face with tousled hair with strands in every direction, huge bags under her eyes, a red nose, chapped lips, and pimples starting to form on her face. She really looked like hell this morning, reflecting her mood from being so despondent about leaving Teddy. What if he never came back to the room and did not see the note? It was a chance she had to take.

She turned on the sink knob for cold water and splashed her face several times. Ahhh. That woke her up. She took a shower and hurriedly brushed her long wavy hair, drying it for a few minutes. It really helped to control the hair strands. If she left her hair as-is after a shower, then who knew how messed up her hair would be in a few short hours?

Teddy, Teddy. Thoughts of him stayed in her mind as she finished up in the bathroom and went to get dressed. She was not in the mood to look chic today so she put on regular jeans, a t-shirt that said "Long Island" in black letters on a blue background, and a sweatshirt. How apropros that her t-shirt would be blue, with blue jeans. She really was feeling down.

It was time to go downstairs and face her family: her mom and dad. She had no siblings, so she had the run of the house when they were not home. It had proven to be a blessing in high school because she was the only one who had parties there and she had her own private bathroom, a luxury none of her friends had at their homes. Her feet made a clunking sound as she walked down the stairs to the first floor.

She could smell coffee brewing -- definitely for her dad, who drank hazelnut coffee every morning religiously before work. He owned his own business. She had worked in his office over a few summers, earning some extra money to go out with friends, plus buy a used 1984 Honda hatchback in a grey color.

She loved that car and had driven it home from Gallaudet just this week. It had only about 25,000 miles on it because she used the Metro system in DC and the subway station was at Union Station. She would go there with Teddy, who also had his own car. They took turns driving there and always went together because parking was so expensive. It made much more sense to use one car instead of two.

As she entered the kitchen, she saw her dad at the wooden rectangular table reading his favorite newspaper, *The New York Times*. It was funny how he could do the crossword puzzle every day with a pen, not pencil. He usually was able to complete the whole thing in less than an hour, even the Friday and Saturday editions, which were much tougher than Monday through Thursday. The only time he had any real trouble was with the Sunday puzzle. Most crossword aficionados struggled with that one and it was legendary how Will Shortz made the clues so devious and tricky to figure out.

"Hi, Dad. How are you?" She glanced at him with a smile on her face. Dad never failed to make her feel special as the only child in the house. Even though he was not affectionate verbally and physically, he remained low-key and collected. It was obvious that he loved her from the way he welcomed her home even though she had come in without much warning. He and Mom had not been judgmental. It was going to be hard to explain why she was home instead of at school the week before vacation, especially during the week.

Her dad wondered what was wrong with Rhonda. Had something happened to her at Gallaudet? She had not given them any warning except for a collect phone call from a rest area on the New Jersey Turnpike. Right out of the blue, the phone had rung and he heard her voice at the office, pleading to let her come home due to a personal emergency. Of course, he had said that was OK, come right home. What else could he have done? He only wanted his daughter to be happy and safe.

Rhonda was his pride and joy. She had been an exceptional student her whole life, excelling in all of her classes. She was in the top ten percent of her class, missing salutatorian by a few percentage points. She really should have won it with the rigorous schedule that she carried during the last two years of high school. The girl who had won with the second highest grade point average had taken some fluff classes to boost her average. Life wasn't fair. But she had definitely done well in college, attending Catholic University on a full scholarship.

As the whole family was devoutly Catholic, he bragged to his friends and anyone within earshot that she attended one of the foremost Catholic postsecondary institutions in the entire country. The only other place he could think of that would make him as proud would have been the University of Notre Dame. He wanted her to meet a nice Catholic guy and he had liked Roy who was her boyfriend now. Hopefully, they would become more serious, to the point of discussing marriage and a future together.

His wife came in. He really loved her. As a college student at Catholic University, he had met her at the library during one night in their freshman year. He had grown up in East Bend, Indiana which was where many Irish Catholics lived. Ironically, she had grown up in Indianapolis which was not that far from his hometown.

As a boy, he had been very athletic and lettered in football and baseball. When he was faced with the prospect of college, he had wanted to go to Notre Dame, but Catholic had offered him a full ride, so that was where he ended up. Thus, he met Esther Bunning, a tall, svelte, beautiful black-haired freshman, while studying at a table in the huge library.

He could remember what happened as if it was yesterday. He had stared at this gorgeous creature across the room for what seemed to be an eternity. Finally, he was snapped out of his reverie by an approaching figure. It was a few seconds until he realized it was her!

"Hi, I could not help but notice you staring at me. Do we know each other?" Her voice sounded so sweet and demure. This was a girl he wanted to get to know better. She was very brave to walk over to him, never having met him before. He gulped before attempting to answer her. He wanted to make a good first impression.

"No, we have never met. But I was attracted to you. My name is Kieran Jennings. I come from East Bend, Indiana." His eyes were mesmerized by hers and for a second she said nothing in return.

"Wow, I am from Indianapolis! My name is Esther Bunning. Who would have known two Indiana natives would meet so far away from home? Mind if I sit here and study?" The corners of her mouth turned upward and she proceeded to sit on a chair across from him.

Kieran thought to himself, *This is good!* After that, the rest was history and they had gotten married upon graduation. He had started his own business selling cars and had done exceedingly well. Thank God for Hondas! He had even given Rhonda a used one for her eighteenth birthday before she went off to college one of those preowned cars that was inspected carefully before he transferred the title over to her.

"Hi, honey. Good morning. Look who's here!" They both looked at Rhonda, who was pouring milk onto her bowl of Cheerios. That was her favorite morning meal and she had eaten that throughout elementary, middle, and high school. Sometimes she would even pour chocolate milk along with regular milk. That always made him chuckle.

Not today though. Just regular milk. That in itself was not unusual, but the way she acted and looked did seem off-kilter. He knew that his wife noticed it too, judging from her upraised eyebrows. His wife was easy to read like a book after twenty-plus years of marriage. He loved her and Rhonda unlike anything else in his life.

Esther Jennings looked back at her husband and felt very lucky to have met him at the Catholic University library. He had been a faithful and loving husband to her all those years. They had a wonderful daughter, Rhonda, who was now in the kitchen eating Cheerios as if this was an ordinary, everyday morning.

In reality, it was not even close to that. She should have been in classes at Gallaudet, where she was taking a leave of absence from Catholic to delve into something called the deaf world. She had no idea what Rhonda had referred to just a few months ago when she broke the news to them about her newfound interest in ASL, some language that deaf people used with their hands through the air.

She had had some concerns because Roy, her new boyfriend, was a full-time student at Catholic and that was across town from Gallaudet. How would he react to her immersion into the deaf community with its sign language? This was something that she and Kieran would have to find out today first-hand from Rhonda.

Even though their daughter was getting a generous scholarship to attend college, their money was paying for her one-semester experience at Gallaudet. They did not want it to go to waste on some wild goose chase for a fad that would quickly dissipate. To their surprise, Rhonda had become a very fluent signer since January and she had kept writing home that she loved it there, mingling with both hearing and deaf friends. Esther was curious as to why Rhonda was home during the middle of the week, though it was not even vacation yet.

Wait a minute. Wasn't there a protest happening at Gallaudet? What was it called? Her eyes darted from Rhonda eating her cereal to her husband who was sitting at the dining table.

"Pssst, honey." She sat down near her husband and poked him in the arm with her right elbow. His face shot up quickly from being buried in the newspaper. "Remember the protest at Gallaudet? Maybe that's part of why she is home now?"

His face furrowed in thought as he considered the possibility. His wife was an astute woman and not much could get past her. Luckily, Rhonda had been an angel throughout her high school years, unlike many of the other teens who had gone to school with her. Was this protest why she was home now?

"Honey..." Kieran started, then stopped in mid-sentence. "Umm... what's that protest called that is happening now at Gallaudet?" He was really curious now and put down the newspaper on the table, smoothing out the pages.

Rhonda stared at Dad. He actually put *The New York Times* down during breakfast time? Now this was a first. Then his question surprised her. Why was he asking about that? Then she noticed that Mom was sitting very close to him and her attention was fully on Rhonda.

Feeling self-conscious standing at the kitchen island, she took a few steps over to the table and pulled out a chair to sit down and put the bowl on a dinner mat. She'd better tell them and get it over with.

"Mom, Dad…do you remember I went to Gallaudet for the purpose of becoming immersed in the deaf community?" They both nodded their heads. A good sign so far. Better plow ahead and tell them the rest. "Well…I broke up with my boyfriend Roy…"

Mom gasped and Dad recoiled backward, almost toppling his chair over. They were both clearly in shock from this news. What in the blazes was going on with their daughter? Kieran looked at his wife and she stared back at him. They'd better find out right now what was going on.

"What? Honey…" Esther stumbled over the words, and she had to take a deep breath. "What happened with Roy? What is going on with you? Why are you home?" She knew she was talking too fast to Rhonda, but her brain was having trouble grasping this new reality of a future without Roy, whom both she and her husband adored. They had met him when they came down to Catholic for a visit just a few months ago, before she decided to attend Gallaudet for the "deaf experience," as she had put it. Their hopes for a future marriage were toppling like a house of cards on sand. She did not like this. Looking at Kieran, it was obvious he was pained by this sudden news.

Rhonda looked at her parents with sad eyes. This was even worse than she had anticipated. They both looked like they were going to keel over. Dad's face was contorted as if he were being tortured in a camp. Mom's eyes were starting to water and her face was becoming flushed. Anytime Mom became upset, her cheeks became red and her nose also. People always teased her about how sensitive she was, easily brought to tears by a movie, even a commercial like the ones from Hallmark. But her mother had a heart of gold and so did Dad.

Even though Dad almost never showed any emotions, he could definitely show pain on his face, and now was one of those times. Rarely had she seen his face this bad. Just like Mom, his face was becoming red. She hoped he would not have a heart attack on them now. His family had a history of heart disease and this emotional stress could not be helping him right now. Better wade in gently and break the news as softly as she could to spare them trauma. Still, better now than hiding it until later. She compared it to how she would rip a Band-Aid off skin. Always better to rip it off and suffer a few seconds of intense pain than to slowly tear the Band-Aid off, prolonging the pain.

"Look…Roy was not the type of man I wanted. I did not know that when I first dated him. Mom, what attracted you to Dad over time?" She smiled through her misty eyes at Mom. Knowing the answer, she had lobbed this softball question so that Mom would be able to correlate with her own personal experience, and so would Dad by listening to the answer.

"Oh, honey, that is such an easy question. Your dad was always so chivalrous with me. He worshipped me anytime we were together. He would tell me how beautiful I was, bought me flowers…" Her face brightened up, remembering what Kieran had done for her. She tenderly looked at her wonderful husband and silently said a thank you prayer to God for having had the temerity to approach him in the library that night when they had first met.

"He is a wonderful, wonderful husband. My best friend. Supports me in everything I say and do, no matter what. We laugh together, cry together. We share our dreams, passions, frustrations every day."

Rhonda sat there, transfixed by what her mom was saying. Why hadn't she heard any of this before? So that was the whole idea of what a true love was. She understood. Finally.

"Mom, Dad. That is not what I am seeing with Roy. So I decided to break up with him last week." Now for the pièce de résistance. "I met a new guy in January. He is so nice, very similar to what happened with you guys." She sighed and paused to gauge their reaction. Hope for the best, prepare for the worst. They just sat there staring at her, mouths agape. Was that good or bad? Let's get moving, more news.

"There's more. His name is Teddy. He is deaf and a special student at Gallaudet, taking classes to get admitted into the graduate program in the deaf education department. He wants to be a social studies teacher, working with deaf students. He is twenty-four, very gener-ous, funny, kind, sweet, and so smart. You guys would really like him!" Her face took on a dreamy expression and she looked at her parents, wondering what they were thinking. Penny for their thoughts. But one more minor detail. Maybe not so minor.

"One last thing…he is deaf."

Kieran heard the word "deaf" and immediately thought, *Oh, no. Not my daughter.* A mute? He had seen them on occasion in different places peddling sign alphabet cards with a pity message on them. What did they usually say? Oh yes…something like "I am hearing impaired and need this money to keep surviving. Please kindly consider donating one dollar in exchange for this card." Something to that effect. But his daughter with one of "them"? No. It was not gonna happen. Over his dead body.

"Did you say deaf, Rhonda? My very own daughter is in love with a mute person? He is deaf and dumb!"

Rhonda was aghast. Did she just hear her dad call Teddy a mute and also called him deaf and dumb? How archaic that was! This myth went all the way back to the Greeks. Plato had said -- along with Aristotle, back then -- that deaf people were incapable of intelligence, based on the use of sign language and the lack of speech! St. Augustine had be-lieved that deafness in a child was the result of the parents' sins prior to their child's birth. The Justinian Code had denied deaf people any property rights. Things hadn't changed until the 1550s when a doctor named Girolamo Cardano in Italy had challenged Aristotle's beliefs.

But her own father, who had professed to be a man of progressive ideas, supporting the ideals of Martin Luther King, Jr., opposed to the idea of her being with a deaf person? Utterly ridiculous! She went on to explain all of this to them and their faces turned from shock to total amazement. She had never felt this strongly about anything in her life up to now. Teddy was the smartest man she had ever known except for Dad.

"Did you know Teddy was a Phi Beta Kappa at college? He graduated cum laude as a political science major. He was in the top ten percent of his public school graduating class! He is definitely not an ignoramus. He speaks and lipreads very well. I challenge you to find me a guy as smart as he is. Plus he is so funny! Please give him a chance!"

Wow, their daughter was on fire right now. Kieran couldn't help but notice her eyes were blazing as she explained the brief history of how deaf people were mistreated. He started to remember what she had told them over the phone in the past month about what she learned in deaf history class. Laurent Clerc. Alice Cogswell. Thomas Hopkins Gallaudet. Abbe Sicard. He was curious what else Rhonda would say to advocate for Teddy and deaf people in general.

"Mom, Dad…I am not done…" Rhonda took a deep breath. Her hands were both flat on the table as she resolved to remain calm with her parents. They were "old school." But that didn't mean they had to remain so. She wanted Teddy maybe to come visit if he did read her letter that she wrote to him before escaping Gallaudet. Sighing, she continued to vent about what she had learned in deaf history.

"The 18th century Enlightenment saw many scholars such as Locke, Rousseau, and Voltaire write about sign language. They never said a word against sign language. It did not matter to them if a deaf person signed or voiced. Reason was possible with anyone if he or she had intelligence. In 1591, Alberti, who was a German doctor, said speech and hearing were totally different functions. He said deaf people could read without learning speech. Deaf education became widespread in Spain in 1620 with the teaching of fingerspelling for religious purposes. In 1760, France saw the first school for the deaf, led by Abbe l'Eppé, using the manual code to teach children who could not hear nor speak. So…"

Rhonda sure had learned a lot in a short time. Kieran was really impressed. Some of the names sounded familiar from what she had told them on the phone. Perhaps he had been hasty in his judgment. Phi Beta Kappa? Heck, even he had not achieved that honor. Yet a deaf man his daughter was in love with had done so!

"Rhonda, can I talk to your mom for a minute in private?" Kieran became quiet and motioned for Rhonda to leave the kitchen by pointing to the dining room hallway. Esther nodded agreement.

What is this all about?, wondered Rhonda. Were her parents going to collude against her wishes and oppose Teddy? Or was her speech enough to dissuade Dad from his outdated views of deaf people? That remained to be seen. "OK, I will go into the dining room and wait for you guys to tell me to come back in."

Having finished her cereal, she pushed herself away from the table. Time for her folks to absorb the news, and discuss with each other what to do. She knew what she wanted. End of story. She remembered Teddy's story about Uncle Benny and vowed that would not happen to her and him. No matter what her parents felt, she wanted to be with him. Every ounce of her body ached for him.

He was such a great hugger, always let her cry on his shoulder. They laughed together for hours. Watched movies on TV together. Laughed and cried at the same things. He was a man who was not afraid to shed tears in front of her. That really appealed to her. They talked about everything under the sun. And the moon too! She wanted to live the rest of her life with Teddy. She wished there was a way to get in touch with him somehow. Hmm. How would she know if he read the letter or not?

An idea occurred to her as she put the bowl in the sink and headed into the dining room. Worth a shot. She darted out of the dining room and went upstairs to her bedroom. Her purse. Where was it? Oh yeah, she had thrown it in the far corner and now it was lying on top of her laundry bag. Some contents had spilled out and were on the floor.

There it was! Her address book, with numbers and names of people in DC.

Maybe someone at Catholic could head over to campus and in all the mayhem check on the status of the note that she had placed on her door. Perhaps he or she could find out where Teddy was and ask what he thought of the note. The very idea of getting another message to Teddy energized her. A notepad, a pen…on her desk! She got to writing, scribbling furiously as she started spilling her thoughts on paper.

Teddy, I am writing this from home. Please, did you get to read my note? I left it on my door with "MOORE" written on the envelope for you and only you to read. I hope nobody else tore it off and read it instead. Just in case, I love you and I want to be with you. I am so sorry for believing what I did. It hit me as I was driving home from Gallaudet. I saw the newspaper at a rest area on the New Jersey Turnpike. Senators and congressmen were speaking out against the Zinser selection. People from all walks of life were furious. I admit, I was wrong…

Where was that newspaper she had bought on her way home? In her knapsack! She scrambled over her bed to the other side and took it out of the bag. Let's see, there it was! William Raspberry, a columnist for *The Washington Post,* had said, "But the students are right in their insistence that if Gallaudet is as good as it claims to be, then it should, in 124 years, have produced a graduate capable of running the place." Profound! William Murchison, a columnist for the *Dallas Morning News* wrote: "The Gallaudet theory of representation is in fact the ghetto theory." Whoa!

Barney Frank, a congressman from Massachusetts had said in the Congressional Record: "For the trustees to turn away from the entirely reasonable request of the students that a hearing-impaired (sic) individual be made president of that college is a very unfortunate expression of insensitivity." She even saw a great cartoon in the paper that had one guy in a white Gallaudet shirt and pants signing "WE SHALL OVERCOME," drawn by Mike Keefe of the *Denver Post*. It amazed her that a cartoonist with no sign skills could depict this powerful three-word phrase so clearly.

So many prominent spokespeople have come out publicly against the Zinser appointment. I was so stupid, Teddy. I apologize for hurting you…never again will I look at Deaf culture with such disrespect. Will you ever forgive me? My number is (718) 555-1144. Please call me through someone so I know you received my note and hopefully the longer letter I left on my door. I hope you want to be with me after everything quiets down, no matter what the result of the protest is.

I love you, with all my heart and soul and body and mind.

Rhonda xoxo

Who could pass the note on to Teddy, whom she could trust implicitly without telling Roy about it? Mentally, she crossed off a few names. What about Sydney, her roommate while she was at Catholic? That was a good choice! Yes! She had grown up in the South and was the ultimate belle. Very prim and proper. Plus, she always kept secrets close to her chest, no matter what people told her in confidence. Rhonda had yet to see her gossip. She was a strong Christian so she hated gossip of any kind.

OK, where was her number…gotta find the last name…first letter "E"…Eamonn! That was it! Leafing through the pages, she got to "E." Yep, there she was. The first entry, Eamonn. Her hands shaking, she walked over to her rotary phone and sat down on the bed. Taking a deep breath, she picked up the receiver with her right hand and placed it under her ear, resting it on her shoulder. With her left hand, she started dialing Sydney's number, one digit at a time. Done!

She could hear the other end ring once…twice…someone picked it up!

"Syd, is that you? Hello?" Her voice definitely sounded tremulous. She was extremely nervous and agitated, thinking what Sydney must be mulling over with the protest and Rhonda leaving their dorm room for Gallaudet.

"RHONDA! Where the heck are you?" Sydney couldn't believe it. After two months of hearing nothing from her former roommate, here she was. What was going on? Boy, Rhonda sounded terrible. Despondent. That didn't sound like her at all. She was very worried now about her good friend, no matter that she had gone to Gallaudet and abandoned the room. She hadn't really abandoned the room. Syd knew she was being melodramatic, but it did feel like she had. Rhonda had every right to follow her heart and dreams. But now she was calling her about something important. She could just sense it. Sydney Marring Eamonn was usually accurate about these things, with her sixth sense.

"Syd? I am so glad to have caught hold of you at school! I am on Long Island right now and I broke up with Roy…"

What? Her roommate broke up with what had seemingly been her perfect boyfriend of one year at school?

"Why did you do that, Rhon? What happened? Why are you not at Gallaudet?" Sydney had not yet really heard about the protest, as she never read the newspaper nor watched the news regularly. Unless World War Three broke out, Syd could not be bothered to read or watch the news. That was just the type of person she was. She didn't want to be bothered with all the bad news that kept coming out, being thrown in their faces on a daily basis. It wore her down, so she tried to avoid it.

"Syd! You haven't heard?" Rhonda started sobbing. This was Rhonda crying? She never had cried in front of Syd in the year they had been roommates. Not once. Ever. She had been like the Rock of Gibraltar for any of her friends who came crying to her. She had such a big shoulder while she was at Catholic. Now this was a totally different

Rhonda whom she had ever met before. She wondered why the tears were flowing. It must be something really major. What had happened in the past few days to trigger this for her former roomie?

"My God, Syd, you really need to read the newspaper, or even watch the news more. Gallaudet University, remember, I am an exchange student there – there was a big protest from Sunday to now about the hearing president that the board of trustees picked. Students, faculty, alumni, and many others are up in arms about this. I just came home from there because I was talking against the protest and thus became persona non grata..."

Syd could hear the sobs in Rhonda's voice as she explained what had happened. But breaking up with Roy? What could that possibly have to do with Gallaudet?

"Wait, wait...Rhon, I don't understand. You talk about breaking up with Roy -- then the next second, you talk about this so-called protest at Gallaudet. What's the connection between the two?" Syd was puzzled and wanted to find out more.

"Syd..." Rhonda was losing patience with her friend, who really should have been keeping up-to-date with what was going on around her. After all, she was a college student and a grown adult.

"My boyfriend Roy was not making me happy. I started at Gallaudet, became immersed in the deaf culture there, forgot all about him. Met a new guy, deaf. He makes me feel so special and cherished in many ways that Roy never did -- plus Roy took me for granted all the time. No flowers, never telling me I am beautiful. I deserve more!"

Syd nodded sagely even though Rhonda could not see her do so. She could understand this part of wanting to be treated like a princess. Heck, any woman with decent self-worth wanted the same thing. Every women's magazine had cover stories about self-esteem, domestic abuse, and that kind of thing. But what about the protest? Coming home out of the blue during the week -- and a week before official vacation started?

"Rhon, OK, I get that part, but I missed a page here. Back up — what is this protest all about?"

"Students want their new hearing president, Elizabeth Zinser, removed because she has no concept of what the deaf world is about. Doesn't sign at all. They want a deaf president and I made the biggest mistake of my life just this week..."

More sobs on the other end. Syd sighed and felt sorry for her good friend. Rhonda did not deserve whatever had happened. But what DID she do?

"Rhon, what did you do anyway that was so bad? Biggest mistake of your life? Aren't you being melodramatic here?" Definitely. What could she have done? The only thing Syd could think of was cheating on a test and getting kicked out of school. Pregnancy? Nah. Not her. She was careful about that kind of thing. Killing someone? Ha, right. That would not be in the realm of possibility.

A pause ensued and Syd wondered if Rhonda had hung up, but she could hear the raspy breathing. Poor Rhonda, whatever she had done was really bothering her and it was taking her some time to gather herself. This was nowhere near the same Rhonda she had known who was always calm, cool, collected. People had actually debated whether Rhonda had any emotions. They called her the Spock of Catholic University. They teased her about doing a "mind meld," which was Spock's way of putting his hand on another person or being's face to see their memories. Only a Trekkie would know that, and Syd was a self-confessed one.

"The protest...Teddy...let me start again..."

Teddy? Who was Teddy? This threw Syd for a loop. Wait a minute! A new guy? During the protest?

"Rhonda, who is Teddy?"

"That's the deaf guy that I met at Gallaudet when I started there. We became good friends -- then great friends. Earlier this week, I told him I supported the Zinser selection and he flew off the handle. I could see that he was very hurt. Let me explain. He grew up in a hearing family that did not sign and still does not today. He's been left out of many dinner conversations and family events. For me to support a hearing president of Gallaudet University who does not sign was like a slap in the face to him. Only now do I realize what I have done."

More sobs on the phone; Syd could hear them. Ahhh … this was slowly coming together. So, Teddy had shunned Rhonda because of this apparent insult to his identity as a deaf person.

"Rhon, do you have strong feelings for Teddy? Is that why you are so upset?"

"Oh yes, that's right. I realized that Teddy was the true love of my life that I had been looking for. We are so perfect together. I knew I had to dump Roy last week, but I was not thinking when I said those things backing Zinser. I am afraid I have lost Teddy for good. But…I wrote a note, left it on my door in the dorm for him. It says "MOORE" on it, as that's my secret name for him. Can you do me a HUGE favor? I would owe you forever and evermore!"

An envelope, "MOORE" written on it, waiting for Teddy? Wow. This was something else. She had a feeling Rhonda wanted her to go over to Gallaudet and check on that.

"Let me guess, Rhon. You want me to check on that envelope and see if Teddy read it or not?" Syd was pretty good about hunches and this would probably be what Rhonda was asking her to do.

"YES! Would you? Pleasepleaseplease? I wish I could do it, but I am at my parents' house now for a few days. It would mean so much to me! Could even save my relationship with Teddy!" Rhonda was hopeful that Syd would be willing to brave the crowds and go over to the Gallaudet campus.

"An idea, Syd. You could make a sign supporting the Deaf President Now movement, DPN for short. It would be easy for you to get on campus with a placard like that. Then hop over to Clerc Hall — it is the one behind Benson, off-white color, not red bricks. My room is on the fourth floor and all you need to do is check to see if the envelope is on the door. If it is, then Teddy doesn't know how I feel about him at all. If it is not there, then two possibilities...he took it and read it, or some other person tore it off and got rid of it."

Rhonda definitely had thought this through! Sure, Syd was a good friend and would do this for her.

"I want a front seat at your wedding, Rhon! Only then will I do this for you!" Syd smiled as she could hear a more quiet presence on the other end of the line. Rhonda was not panting or wheezing anymore. This meant she was calming down.

"Ha ha -- sure, you got the front seat! We will toast you at the reception for saving us if we do get married." Boy, was she lucky to have a good friend like Sydney. Maybe all of this would work itself out eventually. A slight glimmer of hope permeated her being. She now had reason to hold out hope for her and Teddy.

"Syd, if the envelope is not there, please tell Teddy how I feel, that I love him and give him my parents' phone number. You have it, don't you? I saw you write it in your address book when we first met as roommates. He lives in Cogswell Hall, second floor, room 204. Just slide a short note under his door and tape the same note to his door. Please make sure he gets it!"

"All right, Rhon. I will do that today. Don't worry. Just focus on getting yourself together before you come back to DC and face everyone there. What were people treating you like after your opposition to the protest?"

Rhonda shuddered at the memories of how people shunned her after Teddy told Howie what happened with them. For the deaf world, gossip spreads very quickly -- even more so than in the hearing world, for a variety of reasons. Everyone was closely knit together, and the number of deaf people was much smaller than general society, so news traveled much faster from person to person.

It was much worse now with the advent of TTY's. Who knew what the future would bring? Computers were starting to sprout all over campus, especially in the computer lab. She would not be surprised to see someday a communications system that would make typewriters and snail mail completely obsolete! That day was not going to come for a while, but she could see the technological possibilities when computer capabilities became much more complex.

"Syd, it was horrible! I had to order take-out because I was not able to walk anywhere on campus without many people giving dirty looks or glares. It felt so uncomfortable."

Poor Rhonda. She really should have called her and stayed in their old room at Catholic. "Rhon, you could have come here! We would make you feel welcome and you would be safe for the time being. Why did you drive all the way to New York? You can come back here and stay with me. Promise me you will think about it!" That would be exciting, the two of them together again, even for a short period of time.

Rhonda felt better. Sure, she could drive back to DC and stay with Sydney. That would be much safer, and she would be close to Gallaudet. Maybe she could see Teddy again and beg for his forgiveness!

"Thanks, Syd. I definitely will take you up on that offer. I gotta talk to my parents first about Teddy. My dad called him a 'mute' and did not seem happy about me seeing him rather than Roy."

Sydney gasped. She was surprised that Rhonda's dad would label a deaf person with such ignorance. He was supposedly a modern man with ideas and views that were tolerant of anyone, no matter what race, handicap, gender, age, etc. This was very disappointing for her to hear. Rhonda must feel terrible about how her parents viewed Teddy. She herself had never met him, but he seemed like such a nice guy.

"Rhon, I would love to meet him when you come back to DC. Why don't you drive back tonight? You can sleep here as long as you need to. I will get you a copy of my key and you can make yourself at home."

That would definitely work, thought Rhonda. Time to go downstairs and talk to her folks. Let Sydney get that note to Teddy and check on what happened with her envelope with the letter inside.

"Thanks for helping me out so much, Syd! I feel a lot better. Let me know what happens with the note on my door and also alert me if you get ahold of Teddy."

"Sure thing! I am too happy to help. Maybe Teddy has a friend who can teach me sign language. What's it called…ASL?"

They both laughed, thinking about a double date. They often could read each other's minds, as they had become very close friends as roommates.

"Goodbye, my dear roomie!" Sydney exclaimed. She was happy that she would see her friend again very soon. Time to get her room squared away to make space for her to sleep on the floor, and put some clothes away.

Rhonda smiled, hanging up the phone. What had her parents talked about, she wondered. Time to find out, then head out later back to DC. The drive was hell and she hoped she would not see any traffic, but it was definitely possible. Who knew with the Delaware Memorial Bridge? It was always a tricky situation.

Once, she had gotten stuck in the worst possible traffic jam for hours, coming from New Jersey, and finally when she came to the bridge, she saw an accident on the shoulder. There was no need for people to be rubbernecking, but that was what they always did whenever there was an accident on the roads. That really annoyed her. People needed some excitement, and a reminder of how lucky they were not to be in that accident themselves.

Plus, there was the George Washington Bridge. What a freaking nightmare during the day, a bad dream at night. Traffic there was constant all day so she had to plan on driving over that after rush hour ended. There was no way around it. She could go on Belt Parkway, but that was always a bottleneck also. She'd be better off just to stick with

GWB and hope for the best, take whatever came her way.

While Rhonda was upstairs talking to Sydney, Mom and Dad had a conversation about her dating a deaf man. It resembled a scene from the movie *Guess Who's Coming to Dinner*, a 1967 movie starring Sidney Poitier, Katharine Hepburn, and Spencer Tracy, all in their prime. The basic plot was about an African-American doctor dating a white woman, their meeting with her parents who had serious reservations about the couple, then getting to meet his parents. Both fathers had been adamantly opposed to the match, while the mothers were much more amenable. By the end, everyone was accepting of each other.

"Honey, I want you to keep an open mind. Rhonda is upstairs and I think she has a lot to deal with right now. She does not need to listen to your tirades and references to 'mutes.' That is so outdated. She loves him and we need to accept that. Please, for my and the family's sake?"

Esther was worried for Rhonda's well-being, as she was fragile and did not need to hear her father rail against her dating a deaf man. For all she knew, Teddy was the nicest one to her and treated her much better than Roy ever did. From what Rhonda had told them, he sounded like a very special person, and she looked forward to meeting him someday when she brought him back to Long Island.

Kieran sighed, shaking his head. His forehead was furrowed with lines of worry. He buried his head in his hands. "What are we going to do, Esther? It will be impossible to communicate with Teddy. Or does he speak and lipread very well? Remember that Linda Bove on *Sesame Street*? Or Marlee Matlin in *Children of a Lesser God*? They could not speak very well and were unable to lipread!"

"Let's worry about that when we cross that bridge. For now, let's focus on our daughter's happiness. OK? Can you do that for me, for us?"

"Yes, I definitely can do that. Thank you for encouraging me. I love you and how you take care of me like this. We've been married a long time!" Kieran leaned over and kissed his wife on the cheek. What a lady she was, classy and strong. He was the luckiest man in the world to have her as his wife. She would never leave him, standing by his side for a lifetime. He saw too many of his friends who got divorced for a variety of reasons. Some had been stupid, straying with a mistress or two; others had just seen the love dissipate over the years.

"Wonderful, my dear!" Esther was so proud of her husband. She knew how much he loved her, and he treated her like a queen. She soaked up all his attention and felt very fortunate. All of her friends were either divorced or seriously contemplating a divorce. Some were separated at this time, but thanks to New York divorce law, they had to wait a year or more, then file in court the reason for the divorce. It had to be adultery, abandonment, domestic abuse, living apart, or having no sex for a period of time.

It was funny how New York State was the only state in the entire nation not to have a no-fault divorce law. That made it harder and much more inconvenient to obtain a legal divorce here. Some spouses would pretend to have affairs with legal secretaries or even lawyers, and then tell the judge. Women would get pregnant and even though the baby was the husband's, they would tell the court it was someone else's baby just to get the divorce papers processed.

They looked at each other with love in their eyes. Kieran's hands slid across the wooden table and rested on top of hers. His hands were gigantic and he used to be a football player in high school; plus he was always doing manual labor when he was younger. His build was muscular and everyone had admired him during his whole life.

In spite of that, he had been shy around his wife when he first met her and when they started dating. Now, he couldn't imagine life without her and Rhonda. It would have been so empty and unfulfilling. The past twenty years had been the best of his life. He savored each moment he had with them, knowing it could be their last.

They heard a patter on the stairs. Rhonda was coming down from her room. He was curious what was up with her, whether she would be staying at home, going back to school soon to be with her friends, or transferring elsewhere. Their daughter had grown a lot in the past year, with new-found independence. She was such a hard worker, who did not sit back and let the world serve her. She had no sense of entitlement, which was rare for a kid her age. He and his wife were proud of raising a daughter who believed in the value of money and hard work. Their perseverance had paid off.

He chuckled at the memory of his own parents, spoiling her as grandparents always do. After a few years, he had been forced to step in and ask them to dial down the royal treatment for his daughter's sake. It had worked and now she was a low-maintenance girl who still remained beautiful without makeup or accessories.

Now there was a deaf man in love with her. *Not a mute and not deaf and dumb*, he chided himself. He was prepared to apologize to her. He was proud that she had corrected him and even given him a tongue lashing, gently, about the intolerance he had exhibited during their conversation that morning at the table.

Entering the kitchen, Rhonda was relieved to see her parents just sitting there, hands together on the table. Whatever had transpired during her time on the phone in the bedroom had turned out well. Whew. She wondered how her dad felt about Teddy after their intense chat earlier.

"Tinkerbell..." Rhonda flinched at his use of her early childhood nickname. It all stemmed from her favorite story, *Peter Pan*, a classic children's book about a boy who had never grown up. Peter Pan came to London to visit three children, the Darlings, in pursuit of his own shadow. Wendy, the oldest, had helped him "sew" it back on. Michael and John had gone with them to Never-Never Land, battling Captain Hook and his evil buddies.

What had happened was during the bedtime storytelling, Dad had started calling her Tinkerbell because she was so small and innocent, with a glowing disposition. She had loved him calling her that, and anytime he wanted to say something important, he would start off by saying that name. It was his way of emphasizing that he wanted to get a point across to her, without having to tell her that.

It had bothered her as a teenager when Dad called her that, especially in front of her girlfriends and the guys she dated. She chuckled inwardly at one incident when she brought a guy home with a spiked haircut and what seemed to be a tattoo on his neck. He had been dressed in Goth clothes, all black. Even the sneakers were black with some gray.

When he rang the doorbell, Dad had answered, with her not far behind. The expression on his face had been priceless and she would never forget it. He had told her he was looking forward to meeting this Darien -- then upon seeing him, he had said to her, "Tinkerbell…" She then knew it was useless to see Darien again after that horrible first impression.

"Mom and I have talked about you and Teddy. I am sorry, I was wrong. Especially today, nobody labels deaf people mutes except those who are stupid and ignorant. I am neither, so I should not have said that. You were right to chastise me, and your mother did also, gently…"

Dad paused, glancing at Mom. She leaned over to kiss him on the cheek. "Go on, honey, tell her how you feel. I am proud of you for changing your outlook on Teddy."

"Thanks to both of you, I have become a better man that I ever would have been without you girls in my life. I know you, Rhonda, are now a grown woman, but I will always see you as my little girl. So sue me! We agree that you are free to date anyone you want, as long as his name is not Darien with spiked hair and black attire!"

Rhonda laughed, surprised that her father had mentioned him right after she remembered that day he came over and shocked her parents. Just as well. Teddy was a genuinely nice man who just happened to be deaf. They deserved each other and they would be happy together, just like her parents were. They did everything together at Gallaudet, even moving their schedules around to be at the same table at dinner time and sometimes during lunch. Breakfast was tough, with their morning classes conflicting. He was so good to her.

She loved the way he referred to movies to make a point. That annoyed a lot of people, but not her. For example, he had told her once that he hated going to the beach partly because he was afraid of sharks or jellyfish. He had been stung really badly by a jellyfish when he was in high school. He called it his *Jaws* moment and she knew right away he was talking about that shark cult classic that had been popular in the '70s. Was it that long ago? It was very endearing to her how he did that with movies and even TV show episodes.

There was another example of how he did that. They had been talking about the future over pizza on a Friday night in her dorm room. Nobody else had been around, so they got to talking about really personal issues. She brought up the topic of whether they would end up together one day or would lose touch over the years due to the difficulties of mail.

He then went on to tell her about a *Love Boat* episode that had been his all-time favorite. In fact, that show was indeed the must-see of his week because it was one of the first shows that was closed-captioned in the eighties. He memorized the song and anytime she was upset or crying, he would sing it in a low voice. It never failed to make her stop feeling sorry for herself because his voice was so bad, with a monotone, but she loved it anyway because he was trying to make her feel better.

It had been a thorn in his side that *M*A*S*H* was not captioned on CBS. He had even participated in letter-writing campaigns and picketing at their headquarters in New York City, to no avail. She knew that he would have loved the banter and humor on that show. She tried to fill in the blanks for him when they watched repeats of the show, but it was too hard to really convey the meaning of the innuendo between Hot Lips and Major Burns, plus the quibbling between Hawkeye and his tentmates at the 4077th.

"Rhonda, we are behind you 100 percent with Teddy and whatever you decide to do about Gallaudet." She was brought back to the present, listening to Dad talk to her again after the few seconds' pause. Her father was a brave man to admit his mistakes. Her heart swelled, knowing it couldn't be easy for him and Mom to face the fact that she would be with a deaf man, even though he was intelligent, funny, and spoke/lipread very well. They would grow to love him as a son. She had no doubt about that.

"Dad, that means a lot to me. Thank you!" No more words were necessary. She walked over to him and put her arms around his waist. He was such a big man, and she remembered that when she was a little girl, he had seemed like the giant from the Jolly Green Giant commercials or *Jack and the Beanstalk*. Now, he was just another figure as she had grown into adulthood. But she still looked up to him with admiration and love. He would always be a big person for her with his generosity and humility. She hugged him tightly.

"That means a lot to me, truly. You and Mom have been the best parents. I will always love you. Your example inspired me to accomplish so much in my life. I have rebelled before and I know I was stupid sometimes, but you guys stuck behind me all the way. Thank you! I've decided…"

Dad stepped back and looked down on her with a serious expression on his face. He held her shoulders at arm's length. She could feel the tension building as she paused before telling them her decision to go back to DC that night. Mom looked worried also as she sat at the table, her eyes moistening at the embrace. It was such a cozy kitchen; Rhonda felt very comfortable in there. It was ironic also because deaf people tended to confer in the kitchen like moths to a flame. She had noticed that when visiting deaf people's homes with Teddy.

No matter how big or small the apartment or house was, pretty much everyone stood or sat in the kitchen chatting away. She had even asked Teddy why this was so and he shrugged, not knowing why. She made a mental note to ask him again if/when she saw him again. To see him again would be such a moment.

She had taken him for granted during the past two months and had not realized how much she needed him until she hurt him this week. Just to see him again! She didn't expect him to forgive her, but if he ever did, she would make sure he knew how much she had changed the past couple of days. She wanted to be his everything. She knew that now with an absolute certainty. She had never felt that with Roy.

"...I am driving back to DC tonight. My ex-roomie Sydney, you remember her? She will let me stay with her in our old room at Catholic. I hope you guys understand. I want to find Teddy and fix things if I possibly can. I love him and am gonna try to make my feelings known to him." She stopped and held her breath, waiting for Mom and Dad to react to this news.

Contrary to her expectation, both of them smiled broadly. Mom bobbed her head slowly as she looked at her daughter. Never before had she been so proud of Rhonda. She remembered all the times she had told her friends about this precious daughter with her high school academic awards and work ethic, but this news took the cake. Driving back to find the man that she loved and confess her feelings for him during a campus-wide protest that she had opposed at first? This was brave.

She looked down at the wooden table, gathering her thoughts. She wanted to tell Rhonda in no uncertain terms that she was behind her. "Honey, I am very proud to call you my daughter. You made a decision to go back into the lion's den. You may be ridiculed and scorned, but you are willing to go through that to meet Teddy. I hope you can figure it all out. Please do keep us posted!"

"Of course, Mom! I will call you tonight when I get there and I am at Syd's dorm room. It might take me a long time driving. Who knows about the traffic -- it is a hit or miss."

Dad knew what she was talking about. He had driven that route many times and could recite to them the name of every rest area on the New Jersey Turnpike. Some were better than others. Clara Barton. John Fenwick. Walt Whitman. J. Fenimore Cooper. Richard Stockton. Woodrow Wilson. Molly Pitcher. Joyce Kilmer. Thomas Edison. Grover Cleveland. Alexander Hamilton. Vince Lombardi.

It was interesting how certain individuals were honored. Were they all from New Jersey? He wondered if that was the reason for their names. No matter. The memories were indelible. He could even tell people the date and year of each stop, as he had written it all down in a notebook when he was younger.

Driving the Turnpike was boring, that was for sure. It had been no different when he drove it when he was younger, before he got married and they had Rhonda. He had seen some horrific accidents and gotten stuck in a few seriously jammed traffic snarls. But for the most part, he had been lucky with almost-empty highways all the way from New York to Delaware. Every time he hit I-95 near Baltimore and Dover, he would feel relieved. He often would stop at Christiana Mall right after getting over the bridge, just to treat himself to some dinner and shopping to congratulate himself.

"That's fine, sweetie. We are proud of you for going back so soon after coming here. We really love having you at home, telling us what is going on with you. We will always love you -- and can we come visit you once everything settles down? Also, we will be keeping up with the protest, as it was in the newspaper today. I guess we weren't paying much attention to it..."

It was funny how something was so obvious, like the proverbial elephant in the room. He had seen the headline about DPN, but did not pay any heed to it, even though he knew his daughter was a student at Gallaudet for one semester. There had even been a picture of student protestors with placards. He glanced at it on the table near yesterday's mail. He wished he had been keeping up with it, but now he definitely would.

With his daughter having a personal stake in this movement, it suddenly had become important to him that this protest be resolved as quickly as possible, with the selection of a deaf president. It really was ridiculous after he heard Rhonda's explanation of how deaf people were treated throughout history. Could you imagine Notre Dame having a non-Catholic president? Unthinkable! What about Howard University or Spelman College having a non-black president? That would not make any sense. So, why should Gallaudet be any different from those other colleges?

Those members of the board of trustees had to be ashamed of themselves. They couldn't possibly be unable to comprehend the seriousness of this mistake. They had miscalculated what the reaction of the deaf community would be. He resolved to read that article in the *Times* and go to the store to buy all of the other newspapers so he could bone up on this entire issue of a deaf versus hearing president.

Hmm, there was the local library in Bellerose on Hillside Avenue around 250th Street. That would be his errand today. His mission! He was suddenly very energized to have something new to learn. If his daughter was going to bring home a deaf man she was dating, he wanted to be able to communicate with him, even on a rudimentary level. His daughter signed well in such a short time, so there was no reason why he and his wife could not learn. He would get the information at the library, as there had to be some books about sign language and deaf culture.

Esther could sense something change in her husband. She did not know yet what it was, but he seemed to be moving around with a sense of purpose. Whenever he was deep in thought about something, she knew. She could read him like a book after so many years of being together. This was a welcome thing, as he had seemed laggard and sluggish lately, going through each day with none of the vigor that she had seen in him when they were younger, raising Rhonda, going to neighborhood gatherings.

It had been coincidental that many other families on the same block had kids the same age as Rhonda, so the parents had taken turns hosting events. There was even the occasional block yard sale where everyone pooled together their unwanted junk and split the revenues evenly. They knew each other well. The mothers would go to the nearby park with its playground, letting the kids play on the swing set, gossiping among themselves. Later, as the kids got older, they would instead meet at each other's homes and sit around the kitchen table, talking amongst themselves.

Rhonda felt very relieved that her parents were supporting her in whatever she did, including a return to DC. Suddenly she could see Dad's eyes glint with something, and she did not know what it was. Somehow, she knew everything would be all right, but what was it that her dad was thinking? She had to know.

"Dad, are you all right? What is on your mind? Please tell me. I can see your eyes blaze. I know you too well." Rhonda could see this change in her dad even without hearing him talk about whatever was on his mind.

Kieran was surprised that she had noticed a change in him without any words being said by him. But then again, she had always been very intuitive. It was best to tell her and Esther what he had resolved to do. Maybe they could go to the library with him and help find the resources he needed. Yes, that was a grand idea! It would mean a lot to his daughter and show both of them that he truly had changed his perspective from just this morning. He felt ashamed that he had literally held his nose at the fact that his daughter wanted to date a deaf man.

"I want to go to Bellerose Library today and find some books on deafness. Would both of you come with me? Before you drive back to DC tonight?"

"Dad! I would love to!" Rhonda was thrilled at his question. He was actually going to go do some research on deaf-related issues? She knew Dad. He was the type to grab hold of something he had to do and would not let go until he was completely satisfied with knowing everything about it. This could only be good. He would be exposed to ASL, the culture, history, Gallaudet, everything. She started to smile again as he looked down on her. The corners of his mouth curled upward. Mom looked like she was about to cry. Oh no...not the red nose, cheeks. That was Mom's trademark when she became emotional about something.

"I think it is a wonderful idea, Kieran! Let's all go in a little while. I think it opens at 1:00 today. The staff there are nice. We can ask for help. I've been there before and felt comfortable asking the reference librarian to find a book or resource for me." Her eyes lit up and she wanted to walk over to hug her daughter. She pushed herself away from the table, got up on her feet, and walked around the table toward Rhonda.

"I am so proud of you, my precious daughter. We will all go at 1:00. Is that all right with you? Dad and I really want to understand why this is so important to you."

Rhonda stood there, speechless. Her parents were going to do more than she had ever dared to expect when she told them about Teddy. Even more than Teddy's parents had done when they researched options for their son, who grew up oral without signing at all. In fact, when the doctors and speech therapists had told them not to allow Teddy to learn ASL, they also cautioned that signs would impede him from being able to speak and lipread later in life. His parents had bought the lie hook, line, and sinker.

Growing up, Teddy had had social adjustment issues, as he was frustrated in communication with his family. Nobody learned signs to make it easier on him. From age one, he had a hearing aid with molds and a chest body aid. Speech therapy soon followed that, and he had no rest, as his parents pushed him daily to keep achieving new speech milestones. As a toddler, he underwent the lessons that his mother had learned from the John Tracy Clinic correspondence course, which was based in California. He went to Lexington School for the Deaf in his preschool years; then the family had moved to Boston because his father had been in the Air Force for a couple of years.

Teddy had grown up orally and did not learn any signs until high school. Thus, he did not have any friends and had not dated any girls at all until he was a grad student at Gallaudet now in 1988. In fact, she would probably be his first girlfriend and she knew for a fact that he was a virgin, but even though she wasn't, he would be only the second guy that she would be intimate with.

So, she was not that far ahead of him in that department. She had so much she wanted to share with him. Pillow talk. Sharing moments together. Introducing him to her parents! She had goosebumps just thinking about that when it happened. It would all work out…only if she could find him when she went back.

One thing at a time. Now it was time for her parents to learn where Teddy came from, what was important to him and her. It would only improve the relationship she had with them, and deepen the bond they shared. Plus, Teddy would feel more welcome in their home. She wanted that for him. He had spent so much of his life trying to please his parents. She remembered a painful story he had shared with her from high school.

After so much hard work over the years in a mainstream school, without an interpreter, he had achieved membership in the National Honor Society. He had described the ceremony so clearly to her that her heart broke when she heard the story. His parents had been away to Europe for two weeks when word came down who had qualified for the NHS. Teddy received a notice at school and the ceremony was to be held one day at school. His parents were not there. His sisters were too young to understand.

The gymnasium was dark and he was seated all the way in the back, not understanding a thing that was going on there. Names were called. Someone tapped him on the shoulder, pointing to the stage.

Teddy realized it had been his name that was called. Feeling like a freak, he had trudged all the way past the rows of seats, feeling every eye trained upon him. This all meant nothing to him without his family there to share it with him. It should have been a day of triumph, but he felt like an orphan. Just a few days earlier, he had broken down crying, trying to convince them not to go. They told him to calm down and not cry like a baby.

So, he had gone up to the stage to accept the certificate of achievement, and he stood up there seeing everyone applaud. But he felt empty inside, feeling unappreciated. His parents were halfway across the globe going on their merry way, as they did every year. They went to a different country each year. He had hated the old woman who came to babysit for him and his two sisters. She was a chain smoker who did crossword puzzles all day, every day. She was a darn good cook though. He had to give her that. He was a terror in the house, mercilessly berating and picking on his two younger sisters. His grades plummeted every time they went away.

When he told her that story, she had cried shamelessly. She had hated the idea of Teddy feeling so alone, isolated, and overlooked by everyone in his family. He had told her once that he felt that he was a lamppost in the room that everyone saw but didn't really notice was there. They had no use for it, as it was daytime. They walked around it, never acknowledging it was there. He felt frozen, unable to communicate his feelings to anyone because they had not stopped to listen to him at all.

Story after story, her heart felt pierced by each detail that he shared with her over the days, weeks, and months they spent together in their dorm rooms and TV lounges. There was never anyone around them when they had these deep conversations. She wanted to protect him from future hurt because she cared so much about him, and now loved him as she had never loved any man before.

"That is great! Let's all get ready and leave in about half an hour." It was 12:30 and she wanted to get them to the library when it opened so the librarian would be free to answer questions and help them find the resources they needed. She wished there was some way to get the information on those new computers, but for now they would have to get it in person. Wouldn't it be cool to be able to stay home and just be able to find the info on some kind of computer network? That would be far in the future, if it ever happened.

The three of them got ready and before they knew it, the small hand on the grandfather clock struck one, and there was a loud chime. *Funny, Teddy would not be able to hear that,* Rhonda mused. She remembered once they had been in a Jack in the Box and she was swaying to music. He had been sitting across from her, about to bite into a burger. He used to love eating there until he started to feel nauseous after eating their burgers. They were indeed delicious, but what happened afterward had deterred them from eating there again.

He had not bitten into the burger; then he put it down and asked her what she was swaying to. She smiled and said, "There is music coming from the ceiling. I know you cannot hear it. But everyone listens to it. They always play music here. I think it is soothing."

"Music? From up there?" Teddy had looked up, his mouth wide open. He told her his family had eaten at Burger King many times when they were very young. His parents never told him about any music. He had recalled that his sisters were mouthing words to something and it had seemed like songs to him. Then he had looked around for a DJ or some kind of band, but of course there wasn't one. He then had figured out his sisters were just remembering songs from the radio that they had listened to. Imagine, it had not been until he was in his twenties that someone had told him about ceiling music.

That really riled her, the fact that his family had not shared something like that with him. There were so many stories. He practically could write a book about it, and he probably would someday. It would be like the t-shirt saying: "My family went to Europe and all I got was this lousy shirt," or something like that. Every time they watched TV when he was growing up, he had asked his sisters and parents what the characters on TV were talking about. Without fail, they told him they would share the information with him later. Of course, they never did. Teddy had three phrases that really pushed his buttons: "It is not important," "I will tell you later," and "Forget it." If anyone said one of those to him, he shut down immediately and it was hard to pull him back out of his funk. She had made the mistake once and she never forgot it.

"Ready, Tinkerbell?" Dad walked over to her and put his arm around her. Yes, she had never been so ready in her life. They walked outside to Dad's car and she got into the back seat on the driver's side. Mom sat in the front, with Dad driving. He always drove! He was a terrible backseat driver, plus he was so good at finding a parking space. Everyone said that if there was a parking space lottery, he would have been a millionaire many times over! Off they went — she was nervous that this would be a passing fad for them, but it wasn't. They spent two hours in the library, as her parents applied for a new card in the Queens Library System. They learned how to fill out a book reserve form, as there were many other branches with books that Bellerose did not have in its own branch.

She watched as her parents leafed through the various books they had found at the library. One book that she was very familiar with was *The Phrase Book of American Sign Language* by Lou Fant. This was, in her opinion, an excellent source of everyday expressions, providing a fast guide for them to be able to converse in simple conversations with Teddy. Lou Fant himself was a CODA, child of deaf parents, but he was hearing himself. He had been a consultant for the movie *Clan of the Cave Bear*. He also had helped various TV personalities with their need for ASL as part of their shows: Henry Winkler, Diane Keaton, and Mare Winningham.

Another book they found was *Changing the Rules* by Frank Bowe,

with a foreword by Senator Bob Dole. This was an excellent autobi-
ography which had many details very similar to Teddy's stories that
he had told her. Bowe had become a professor at NYU, and she had
always wanted to read this book. It was good that the library had it,
so now she could go back to Gallaudet and borrow a copy either from
the library there, or from someone else. Maybe Teddy had a copy of
the book himself!

She was excited for her parents. But it was time for her to pack
and get ready to go back to DC. She felt ready for whatever came
her way. Did Syd ever catch Teddy on campus like she asked her to? It
would have to wait until she arrived at Catholic. She was viewing the
return with trepidation, but she knew she had to go back if she wanted
any chance of a reconciliation with Teddy.

Suddenly, she realized there had to be newspapers in the library.
She ran over looking for the newspaper section near the magazines.
There they were, all piled up. The *Times* had that article about the
protest, and there was something in another newspaper outlining how
Zinser had been learning ASL, hoping to get a working knowledge by
the time she started working as president of Gallaudet on July 1st,
1988. What a joke! Everyone knew it was nearly impossible to grasp
ASL, with its complex features and syntax, in a few short months. This
woman who had proclaimed she was in charge was seriously deluded.
Why had the board picked her?

There was a radio playing on a long white table near the newspapers. Someone was listening to a local station. Had she just heard
correctly? King Jordan backed the board's selection? What the heck
was wrong with him? She could only imagine how Teddy and everyone
there felt about it. She tried to picture his facial expression, feeling
rejected again like he always did with his family at functions. Poor him!
She hurried over to her parents, who were in line checking out their
books.

"Did you hear on the radio just now? King Jordan just backed Zinser's appointment. Poor Teddy! I really can't wait to get back there and see him in person." Rhonda was downcast and worried about his well-being. Hopefully, Syd would have been able to get word to him before it was too late to repair the damage she had caused. Finally, her parents had the books stamped out with a due date of three weeks. That was plenty of time for them to read these books and if they liked them, they could go to a local bookstore to buy them for reference.

How was Teddy doing right now? she wondered. She tried sending him a telepathic message as they exited the library and turned the corner onto 250th Avenue. They had parked right past the fire hydrant, which everyone hated, because it made for fewer parking spaces on that narrow street. She would give anything to be able to see the scene at Chapel Hall where Teddy and everyone else had found out about King Jordan's betrayal. He did not deserve to be the president with his flip-flop. A man who led a university of the deaf had to be someone of principle, not a wishy-washy person who bucked the opportunity to make a stand for deaf people.

Teddy sat in the cafeteria, silently eating dinner. The usual slop here. Prisoners got better food than they did, for sure. Howie was seated next to him, animatedly waving to everyone to watch the TV right away. He looked up and gasped at seeing Greg Hlibok and Marlee Matlin on the tube, debating the merits of the protest, outlining why the board was so wrong in their selection. Ted Koppel was moderating as host. He asked Zinser point-blank, "Are you a puppet of the board?" Everyone in the cafeteria cheered and hooted when Zinser's face blanched and she took a few seconds to recover.

That was a great question for her! Teddy admired Koppel for having the guts to ask that. Did he actually come up with these questions, or did the teleprompter show them to him? He would have to find out one of these days. Hlibok was more than holding his own with Zinser. At only age twenty, he was sparring with her like a veteran. She was being defensive, saying she was her own free agent. Teddy knew that was a bold-faced lie, as she was being handled by a public-relations firm that had handled many politicians and business people in the past.

He wondered what would happen if Zinser walked into the cafeteria right now. He recalled a cartoon he saw in *The Washington Times* by Bill Garner, showing Zinser tied up to a wooden pole with wood scattered all around her. A lynch mob of screaming, waving people surrounded her, fists in the air. One guy with spectacles and a tie said to her, "They feel you're not the sensitive type, Ms. Zinser!" Another guy was poised to pour a canister of gas onto the wood planks and a woman had a blazing torch. Judging from the mood in the room, he had no doubt that could happen.

That afternoon, after Jordan's stab in their back, things had become tumultuous. Even police cars had a lot of trouble getting through the crowds. He had witnessed one episode himself, when student leaders were escorted off campus for their meeting with Zinser. He saw three deaf leaders in the back with Bridgetta Bourne sitting in the front passenger's seat. The two guys at the windows had their arms outstretched, leaning out, their fists in the air. Everyone went wild when the car passed them. His friend Howie was right near the street, watching them move slowly in the car. It was a defining moment for the protest.

Upon leaving that scene, he passed the large mobile home which sat in front of Fowler Hall at the 8th Street entrance, donated by an alumni couple who supported their cause. This was the new DPN Information Center. He kept walking and went around Fowler toward the bust of Laurent Clerc which overlooked the north side of campus. He could only imagine how Clerc would have felt if he had been alive to see this protest. He would have felt physically ill and very disappointed, like the rest of them. Why was it OK for so many schools for the deaf to be led by deaf leaders before 1880? They had proved their competence in so many ways.

He walked past the Edward Miner Gallaudet Building, where the president's office was. He paused by the front door and could see Ole Jim just across the campus road. Remembering another cartoon he had seen in the papers, he saw himself with a Gallaudet jacket looking at Zinser's office door, which had the words "LISTENING IMPAIRED" painted on the glass. This was a great drawing by Peter Stenier in *The Washington Times* and it had made everyone laugh when they saw it.

"Hey, Teddy! Hey!" Duh, of course...Howie realized that Teddy didn't have hearing aids on, so he couldn't hear his yelling. Huffing and puffing, he ran past Clerc's bust and College Hall. Finally, he caught up to Teddy and slapped him on the right shoulder.

Teddy was startled and turned around quickly. Howie! How good it was to see him. He really needed his company. For some reason, he could sense Rhonda thinking about him. Dismissing it as his imagination, he put it out of his mind.

"What's up? What's that paper you have in your hand? Is it for you? Me?" He could see the paper being waved in the air right in front of him. Obviously it was for him. But from whom? Then, out of the corner of his eye, he saw a woman standing near Howie. She was very pretty, dressed in preppy clothes, and wearing a dark wool jacket. She had a green beret on her head and she looked nervous, hands in her pockets.

"Teddy..." His eyes darted from Teddy to the girl. "This is Sydney. She was...ahem...Rhonda's roommate at Catholic before transferring here this semester. What I am holding in my hand is a message that she gave Sydney over the phone from Long Island!" He thrust the paper out toward Teddy. "Take it! Rhonda wanted to tell you something!" He nodded vigorously.

For me? Teddy couldn't believe it. *Me? From her?* Ah, she must have not known if he got the other note taped on her door. This was the Sydney that he had heard about from Rhonda, huh? She definitely was very pretty. But nervous. He better take that note before it flew away in the air, knowing Howie was very clumsy and could accidentally let go of it. His right hand slowly reached out, grasping the paper between his thumb and index finger. It was folded in half and then in half again. "MOORE" was written on it, so it definitely was for him.

He slowly opened it as if in a daze, and his eyes took in every word she wrote. Yes! She was coming back! Sydney had come looking from him on campus to alert him that Rhonda was driving from New York to DC in hope of a reconciliation. His dream had come true. She was sorry for her wrong support of Zinser! Now this was more like it. He was relieved that she had come around. He couldn't wait to see her again.

Sydney came all the way across town just to find him? That must have been a very difficult thing for her to do. He respected her for doing it. Even Howie was treating her with respect, as he realized how much Teddy felt for her after their discussion since reading the letter that Rhonda had left on the door. It was going to be a very interesting night for Teddy, seeing Rhonda again. But he couldn't wait. For so long, he had dreamed of meeting a woman who accepted him for who he was: a deaf person with his own communication needs, ASL, deaf culture, and identity.

"It is nice to meet you, Sydney. Rhonda told me a lot of good things about you. I appreciate you coming all the way here and braving the crowds out front just to find me. How in the world did you find me, anyway? We've never met!" Teddy wondered if she had seen a picture of him from Rhonda. That was possible! Or maybe she had described Howie perfectly to a "T" and saw him outside in the faces that were watching the car go by on its way to meet Zinser.

"Oh, I just asked around with your first and last name on a piece of paper, plus Howie's. Luckily, he was right there and saw what I was doing, so it was easy for me to find him. Then, he started running off and motioned for me to follow him. That was when I saw you walking, and I knew I had found you. I am so glad that Howie was there. You had just walked off so you didn't see me asking around about you."

Teddy stood there, amazed. The power of coincidence! Good old Howie had come through today, big time. He had bailed Howie out with academics, as Howie had a severe learning disability which meant he struggled a lot with math. But with his tutoring, Howie's grades were starting to creep into "B" territory. Before this semester, he had gotten D's and C's in introductory algebra. Now he was doing at least one letter higher in Algebra I. Howie was definitely returning the favor with this one providential occurrence so he was prepared to call it all even at this point.

"Let's go to Union Station for dinner, guys!" Teddy exclaimed. "Dinner is on me! Then we can head over to Catholic and meet Rhonda when she gets here to your dorm. Does that sound good?"

Howie and Sydney nodded. It was funny how Teddy spoke and signed at the same time. Howie laughed because he had never seen Teddy do that before. His speech was really good, because she had understood him with no difficulty. Yet he was able to sign, but in English word order. This was called Signed English, or more specifically, Manually Coded English (MCE) which meant the person signed in the correct English syntactical order, using the same rules as spoken English.

Normally, both Howie and Teddy signed in ASL which had very different grammar rules from English. It was impossible to sign ASL and speak at the same time. The range between Signed English and ASL was called the "Sign Continuum." He had learned about it in his introduction to deaf education class taught by a cool professor at Gallaudet.

They decided to avoid the crowd at the 8th Street entrance, and kept walking past Ole Jim toward 6th Street. The three of them walked step in step. Sydney didn't know this campus at all, so she let Teddy and Howie take the lead. The walk was not far. They made a left when they got to the gate on 6th; then at the corner they could see the crowd a block east, right on Florida Avenue, chanting and pumping their fists in the air. They wanted to get away from that.

Teddy and Howie looked at each other and as if communicating telepathically, they made a 180-degree turn. Sydney followed them, passing the deli on the corner. They walked to New York Avenue, which was a busy intersection with a Wendy's restaurant on the southeast corner. Resisting the temptation to eat there, they kept walking south on New York Avenue. It was a bad neighborhood anyway and the people inside the Wendy's were questionable at best.

It was interesting to Sydney how people walking past them gave them all the space they needed. Was it because the two guys were deaf? It reminded her of a story one of her hearing friends had told her about Great Neck North. A deaf student had attended the high school there from 1978 to 1982. The few minority students often would beat up the white students for no reason, but this particular white guy who was deaf had no problems there. Everyone left him alone and he was given a wide latitude. Why? Because he was deaf. She was seeing the same thing here. No hassles. Wasn't that interesting?

She was fascinated by the constant motion and flow of the guys' hands with no sound coming from their mouths. What the heck were they talking about? They had a wide variety of facial expressions and their eyes would connect on numerous occasions while they walked the short distance to Union Station. She surmised correctly that deaf people placed a high value on eye contact.

Hearing people really didn't care much for that. They had conversations sometimes without even looking at each other. And the facial expressions were unbelievable! Never before had she seen this wide assortment of them in a single conversation. Sometimes, she had thought one of them was mad or upset, but it had turned out to be a false alarm. She wanted to learn all this now. Wait until Rhonda came back! She would ask her to teach her everything. Maybe take classes at Gallaudet. Wouldn't that be cool?

She was falling behind, having been deep in thought. Her pace quickened as she caught up to them. She didn't want to get too far behind, lest some strange guy accosted her here. She had never been this far outside of Catholic University. Michigan Avenue in the northeast part of DC was not a particularly bad area. There were some nice apartments and a Jerry's Sub that she frequented near the campus. But this really was a downgraded neighborhood, so she felt safer walking right next to the two guys even though she was unable to understand their conversation.

Finally, they arrived at Union Station. She decided it was time to call Rhonda at her parents' house. "Hey guys…" Duh. They couldn't hear her. She should have her head examined! What to do? She tapped Howie's left shoulder, a bit too forcefully. They stopped in their tracks. She pantomimed with her right hand in the shape of a "Y" and a duck's mouth with her left to signify talking. They nodded and understood. Whew. She did it! Communicated with two deaf guys. There was a payphone right near the train terminals, near the huge bookstore.

She walked over to a payphone and her hand dug into her pocket for change. Shit! She did not have enough, so she looked at Teddy and Howie. She put her right palm out and pointed at it with her left index finger. They understood right away and immediately searched their pockets for spare change. Oh, why didn't these phones accept credit cards? Teddy came up with three quarters and one dime. Howie was able to rustle up two quarters, three dimes, and a nickel. It wasn't much, but maybe it would suffice for a few minutes. She hoped so, anyway.

She dialed the number for Rhonda's parents and the line rang once…twice…she looked at Teddy's face, full of anticipation. Howie had his right hand on Teddy's left shoulder. What a good friend this Howie was proving to be to him. She mused about what Howie was like as a person. Maybe later she would think about it some more. Someone picked up the phone!

"Hello? Who is this I am talking to?" Sydney hoped it was Rhonda.

It would be awkward talking to her parents.

"Syd! It's me! What is going on? Good news, bad?" Rhonda's voice was very high. Sydney knew that happened whenever she was nervous, so that was not a worry for her to hear.

"Good news, Rhon. I have Teddy and Howie with me!" She could hear a loud squeal on Rhonda's end. She covered the mouthpiece and mouthed, "She's yelling, I think in a happy way." Teddy clapped his hands and signed what she said to Howie, who then smiled at both of them. United in purpose, they felt the electricity in the air and knew that there was a very happy reunion about to happen that night. Syd proceeded to tell Rhonda where they were.

They decided to grab a bite downstairs, so they rode the escalator to the basement. The food choices down there were amazing. Only a few years ago, there had been basically nothing there until a multimillion-dollar renovation transformed Union Station from a barren, old-fashioned stopover to its current status as a top-of-the-line hub with Amtrak and a huge food court, along with a shopping mall with over twenty stores. They agreed to meet at a table near the spiral staircase.

Teddy and Howie zoomed straight to the Rice Bowl. Every time they went to Union Station, they ate there, period. There was no discussion between them. The food there was delicious and very reasonably priced. Sydney had never eaten there. She figured she could try it, so she went with them. After getting their food, they sat down at a table and silently ate. So much had happened that day and they were already wiped out from the bubbling emotions. There was much more to come before the night was over.

Rhonda sat in her driver's seat, zooming down the Turnpike. She had left just an hour ago. Her parents had been sad to see her leave so soon, but they made her promise to call them as soon as she arrived in DC. One of her good friends had been killed in an auto accident when they were in high school together. That was why they never took for granted that their daughter would arrive safely. It was a steadfast rule in the Jennings household that anyone driving had to call upon arriving safely at the destination. That applied to plane flights, train rides, anything. Even a bike ride! But she respected this, because it gave her folks peace of mind.

Her dad knew all the rest stops so he had told her which ones to go to and which to avoid. It was funny to her. But he was right, as she had tested each rest area over the months and saw what he was talking about. Tonight, she was too keyed up to stop anywhere. She had made sure to fill up the gas tank before leaving so she could drive straight through the Turnpike and leave nothing to chance. She had even gotten an oil change and her tires checked after the library visit.

Teddy! She was going to see him again tonight. She wanted to hug him, kiss him, tell him he would never be alone ever again. He deserved her, she deserved him. End of story. Rolling down her window, she could feel the spring breeze in the air. It was a little chilly, but that was to be expected at night during March. It felt good and she let her hair float around in the car. That made her feel a little daring, as she was about to take a leap of faith returning to DC, even though she knew Syd was with Teddy and Howie right now in Union Station eating. Probably the Rice Bowl! She chuckled, thinking about Teddy savoring the chicken with noodles. He ordered that every time they went. Plus a Coke to wash down the food. He was so predictable!

She loved him anyway. Every mannerism. Even the way he said the word "fabulous"! When they had first met at that party then the security office, she had to get used to his speech because it was with what he called a "deaf accent." She had laughed at that phrase, not to mock him, but to appreciate the way he kept a positive outlook on his deafness in spite of being isolated from his family and their gatherings.

After a few days, she could understand pretty much everything he said to her out loud, and then one day they had talked about ordering ice cream at Union Station. When the counter person had told him that he could have chocolate sprinkles and whipped cream on his sundae, he said, "That would be fabooolous!" She had cracked up laughing and tears lined her cheeks. He had looked at her and said, "What's wrong? Did I say that the wrong way?"

She had looked at him and shook her head, smiling. "No, it was just so cute the way you said it with a long 'u' drawn out. I loved it!" He looked relieved and they went ahead to eat the ice cream at a nearby table. Ever since then, she had asked him to say that word anytime she wanted to smile and feel better. He took it good-naturedly. It became a private joke between them that nobody else knew about. So, the first thing she was gonna tell him was to say that word again!

Trees and telephone poles whisked by her as she kept driving. Ah, there was a sign for the Delaware Memorial Bridge, twenty miles away. She had made good time! It was only 9:30 and she had seen no traffic yet, even over the George Washington Bridge. It was like everyone knew she was being reunited with Teddy so they stayed out of her way, like Moses parting the Red Sea. She chuckled at another memory of Teddy, who told her that this parting of water was an extraterrestrial event, an obvious example of gravity control. He was full of surprises.

In high school, Teddy had written an essay on the topic of his own choice. He struggled in eleventh grade English with a strict taskmaster who gave him no leniency with weekly essays in class and for homework over the weekend. He had gotten his first C's in the fall quarter, and that upset him so much. But as the year progressed, his grades crept up into A and B territory. As a reward for his hard work, he was allowed to write about anything for the last assignment of the year. She shuddered at what had happened then.

Teddy had sat down at his mother's typewriter from the 1950s and whipped up an outstanding essay that was lucid and captivating. He had shown it to her not long ago, as he kept it as a memento from high school days. He showed it to his father, who immediately forbade him from handing in this essay because of his strong Catholic beliefs, no matter how well it was written. He had gone in depth about Erich von Daniken who wrote the infamous bestseller, *Chariots of the Gods?* in the seventies.

This devastated Teddy to no end. He was forced to hold onto this masterpiece (at least she thought it was that good, but to each his own) and type up something about a boring topic: the human heart. He did a good job and received an A-minus. But he had never forgotten this episode and it was one of the most painful memories he had from his younger days. She flinched when he told her every little detail, including the way his dad had mocked the idea of extraterrestrials intervening in human history. Why was that so ridiculous? It was not any more silly than angels coming down to earth to inform Mary of Jesus' birth.

Toll-booths appeared in her line of vision. She got her purse out and was ready when she drove up to the collector. It was amazing how there was nobody on the road now. That was always a good thing. The car's tires made quite a noise as she went over the bridge. It was a beautiful view of the water. She imagined herself and Teddy canoeing down the Delaware River one day. There were so many trees. She could see the stars in the sky tonight. Just two more hours and she would be there at Union Station. They had changed their plans from Catholic because it would be easy to meet at the McDonald's at the far end of the train hub there.

An hour later, she could see the Baltimore lights fast approaching. There was Inner Harbor, but it was not visible from I-95. She had gone there with Teddy for a very short time just to take a look. It was cold outside. He had been such a true gentleman that day, making sure she was warm enough, even offering his own coat when she was shivering. So many memories in just two months with Teddy, and they were not even dating yet!

The McHenry tunnel loomed ahead. She did not like going through it, as she had a slight case of claustrophobia. But she forged ahead and made sure she did not change lanes. It was forbidden there and she did not want to get a ticket, which would delay her arrival at DC. After a few minutes, she breathed a sign of relief as her car exited and then she saw the sign for 295. Taking that, she kept going. Only half an hour left! Hopefully, Sydney was doing OK with Teddy and Howie, communication-wise. How did she feel about sign language after spending time with them? She wondered about that. She'd definitely ask her later.

Howie glanced at the digital clock at the Amtrak terminal. They were seated at the McDonald's which was the agreed meeting place. Teddy looked nervous. His feet rocked under the table. Howie put his right hand on Teddy's forearm.

"Relax, man. She will be here soon!" He looked at Sydney, and motioned to ask if she wanted anything from the counter. She shook her head and mouthed, "Thank you." He had really been wrong about Rhonda. When he first met her in January, he thought she was a snob from Long Island who felt she was too good for the deaf world. She had been nothing but nice to him this whole time.

This experience during the protest, watching Teddy read that letter she left on the door, plus getting to know Sydney a little bit, Howie felt very humbled. He knew he had been wrong. He would apologize to her the first chance he got. The same for Teddy. He would respect his friend's relationship with her even if it meant they had less time together as best buddies playing DOOM or going to Laurel Racetrack. The ecstatic look on his face had been priceless for Howie to see when Sydney had appeared in front of Teddy at Gallaudet. There had been such a transformation in his friend over the past couple of hours.

It was now 11:00 and McDonald's would soon be closed for the night. They could always sit at the last gate for the Amtrak trains. It was open twenty-four hours a day for incoming and outgoing trains. So, no matter what, Rhonda would find them because they would be sitting right in front of McD's and there was no way to miss them. Howie's eyes couldn't believe what he was seeing. Was that Rhonda coming down the stairs far off? He had been blessed or cursed (depending on how one looked at it) with better than 20/20 vision. He called it his "hawk vision" and Teddy had laughed about that.

"Psst, Teddy..." He nudged Teddy, who was half asleep on the chair next to him. "Look! Guess who is coming our way?"

Teddy sat upright quickly and he took a few seconds to get his bearings. Rhonda? Did Howie just tell him she was coming? Where? His eyes roamed the Amtrak gate area and suddenly he could see her black wavy hair at a distance, passing the shoeshine booth right before the newsstand. Rhonda! He pushed his chair away and started running toward her. Not a moment to waste! His feet couldn't move fast enough and she was getting closer by the second. She saw him, and her eyes lit up immediately.

Teddy! She dropped her suitcase and started crying, her arms outstretched. He embraced her and held her tightly against him, raising her several inches above the ground. Oh, Teddy! It was so good to be with him again. He was definitely crying also. His face nestled into her neck and she loved it when he did that with her every time they had said hello or goodbye. She sobbed and kissed him on the cheeks. She was so happy at this moment, as she had never thought they would be reunited like this!

He felt like the luckiest man on earth, hugging and embracing Rhonda. Like her, he had never expected this to happen. If you had asked him a few days ago if he envisioned ever seeing her again, he would have adamantly said "no" with no equivocation. Yet this was happening right here, right now! Life had a way of throwing curveballs when one least expected it.

"I am so happy to see you, be with you, Rhon!" Teddy could barely see her through his tears. She wiped his cheeks and under his eyes. He took his right arm off her and took his glasses off, blinking rapidly to get the water out. She had been crying also. His left arm went over her head and he put his left index finger under her left eye, wiping away the moist tears there, then he did the same with her right eye. They started laughing together because they were wiping each other's eyes. How cute was that?

Howie and Sydney stood off to the side near the McD's entrance, giving them the space they needed. Then, as if by mental command, they walked toward Teddy and Rhonda. As they got closer, Rhonda turned her head and saw them coming. She laughed and stretched her arms out for Sydney. Her best friend in the whole wide world had really come through big time for her. She would forever be in Syd's debt for doing this to get her and Teddy back together.

"Excuse me, Teddy – let me go hug Syd, OK?" She looked at Teddy apologetically and he nodded, gently nudging her toward Sydney. That was all the encouragement she needed. They hugged tightly for a few seconds, crying in each other's necks.

"Thank you so much, Syd! I can never repay you for such a big favor! Without you, I would never have seen him again!" Then, she stepped back and signed to Teddy what she had said to her just now. She firmly believed in making sure that he knew what she said to anyone. It reminded her of a story he had told her about a date he had in January when he first came to campus.

A hearing grad student took him to meet her parents on the way home from a party. She had talked to her folks for forty-five minutes without interpreting for Teddy. He felt terrible, just like he did with his own family. When they left her parents' house, he told her he would never date her again because she forgot all about him and was not sensitive to his communication needs. She was a very good signer -- not fluent, but she could easily have interpreted the whole conversation among them. But she did not do that. Rhonda had vowed to always make sure Teddy was part of any conversation she was in.

The tears dried up and the four of them got together in one big hug.

Even Howie, who was never demonstrative of his feelings and emotions, took part. It was a unifying moment for them. Time for reality to set in. They went off to drive to Catholic and avoid the hoopla that was fast becoming the norm at Gallaudet. They agreed to meet again on Thursday morning at Union Station. Teddy knew where Rhonda and Sydney would be coming from, as he had gone to their dorm several times before by train, then a short walking distance from the Metro stop. Tired from the events of the day, the four of them went to bed and quickly fell asleep.

Chapter Five:

Thursday, March 10th, 1988

O n Thursday morning, Teddy woke up and followed his usual routine, meeting Howie in front of the cafeteria at 8:00 a.m. to head out to Union Station again. They usually had breakfast together in the cafeteria, but not today. They walked across campus and then trekked the fifteen-minute distance to meet the two girls at the same McDonald's. Upon entering Union Station, Teddy wanted to see the latest newspaper and find out what was going on with the protest in the media.

"Howie, did you see this? Look! Congressman Bonior on the front page of *The Washington Post* comments about federal funding of Gallaudet and how it could be seriously affected by Zinser's refusal to step down!"

They became excited and Teddy went ahead to buy the newspaper. He actually bought two copies, as he planned to start a scrapbook when all of this was over. This was a once-in-a-lifetime experience that he definitely would never go through again. You just could not buy this kind of first-hand experience anywhere, ever.

They walked over to the McDonald's and knew they were early by a few minutes. They were supposed to meet Rhonda and Sydney at 9:30 a.m., so they sat down with their Egg McMuffins and hash browns and started eating. Teddy opened the newspaper to read more about Bonior's statement and Howie peered over to read along with him. It turned out that the faculty at Gallaudet had voted 147 to 5 on Wednesday to support the students' demands. Five faculty members should be fired! Teddy wondered who they were and how they could live with themselves. No matter. The students were winning and nobody could turn back the momentum now.

He couldn't imagine how Zinser was feeling with the pressure surrounding her. Would she resign today? Tomorrow? He believed that it was just a formality at this point. She had been so determined on Sunday and Monday to take up the reins at Gallaudet, and now he doubted she had anywhere as much resolve as she did a few days before. Did Howie agree with him?

"Hey man, can you believe how fast things are happening? What do you think Zinser is feeling right now?"

"Teddy, I have no idea, but I can tell you this: she feels lousy! Nobody really prepared her for the intensity that this movement would bring. I think your roommate Luis told everyone before Sunday that this would happen and we all laughed at him. He turned out to be right!"

They thought back to the rally the Tuesday previous to the start of the protest. Teddy had been there and was photographed for the newspaper while Howie sat in the stands watching it happen. His only regret was that Howie did not stand beside him during the rally so they could be photographed together. It would have made for a nice picture in his future scrapbook about the entire experience. He hoped that they would stay in touch for the rest of their lives, but who knew what would happen after graduation. Sometimes people went their separate ways. It was hard staying in touch via phone and mail.

There was Rhonda with Sydney! Teddy smiled and stood up while Rhonda walked over and hugged him tightly. They kissed on the lips and embraced. Never again would there be any doubt about anything between them. Teddy suddenly had a thought about meeting her parents. He felt apprehensive about the whole idea, but he forced himself to relax and put it aside. First, they needed to finish the protest and clean up after the mess that the board had left them with.

Sydney was reeling from everything that Rhonda had shared with her last night. Even though they were tired from such a long day, they had been unable to sleep. So, Rhonda told her about what her parents did at the library and the discussions they'd had the whole day. It seemed that her father had really accepted the situation about their daughter and Teddy. It was to their credit that Rhonda was able to come back to DC with peace of mind. She had her best friend back! She had even learned the ABCs and was eager to try it on Howie, who had shown a lot of patience with her the night before while waiting for Rhonda to arrive.

"Teddy, guess what? Syd knows the alphabet now and she really wants to learn to sign. Howie, would you be willing to teach her as we go along?" She looked at Syd, who nodded agreement. Howie's eyes opened wide, and his mouth formed an "oohhh." He quickly recovered and said, "Sure! I would be glad to!" He glanced at Teddy, who was smiling and shrugging his shoulders. It looked like the four of them would be sticking together for a while.

"Did you hear the news about Gallaudet today?" Rhonda was excited. King Jordan was going to make an announcement that afternoon and everyone was saying that he was going to do a 180, abandoning the board and Zinser. People reportedly had been approaching him left and right. She had even heard people talking at Catholic and Union Station while she walked around with Sydney. That was one of the benefits of being a hearing person! You could eavesdrop innocently on any conversation within earshot. She wondered what Teddy would think of this news development.

"Are you kidding me? Today? I bet he will change his stance. He has to if he wants to keep any shred of decency for himself!" If he did not do that, then he was finished as a leader in the deaf community. There was no way he would be able to feature prominently among deaf people after appearing weak by being perceived as a slave to the board that whole week. With so much support behind the protest, why would Jordan want to stick to the losing side, especially if it was in the wrong?

They discussed among themselves what to do and decided to just walk around Washington Mall. It was such a beautiful place and it never failed to soothe Teddy's mind whenever he was thinking about something. He had gone a couple of times with Rhonda. The last time had been just a week or two ago when the weather warmed up to around fifty-five degrees.

"Rhonda, do you remember the deaf peddler we met the last time we walked at the mall? Wasn't that really something?"

"How could I forget, babe?" It felt good calling Teddy such an endearing nickname. She had wanted to do that for so long, but knew it had not been appropriate yet while they were "just friends." Now that they knew their feelings for each other, it just felt natural for her to do that. She knew he liked that. She knew him so well by now and it was going to be the best thing for her to be dating her best friend other than Sydney.

Babe? Teddy chuckled. He did like that, recalling that he had mentioned to Rhonda a couple of times how he was so corny with nicknames and monikers, it was obvious she had not forgotten. That was one of the nicest things about being with her, talking to her. She rarely forgot details. Maybe once in a while that would come back to bite him you know where, but for the most part it made for a nice feeling inside him that she had been paying attention.

They spent a few hours walking along the side of the reflecting pool, going into the Jefferson and Lincoln Memorials, waiting in line for the Washington Monument, visiting the newly built Vietnam Memorial, and sitting on a bench chatting. It had been a challenge for Rhonda to interpret for Sydney and Teddy and Howie, but it was worth it for her to see everyone enjoying the company.

Syd had even learned a few new phrases, such as WHAT-UP, MY NAME SYDNEY, YOU AGE WHAT?, GALLAUDET, ME HEARING YOU DEAF. Syd obviously was enjoying herself and had even commented that she wanted to transfer to Gallaudet for one semester or one year like Rhonda had. Was it her imagination, or were Syd and Howie starting to cozy up to each other as if they were dating?

Howie was not bad-looking and with a woman's help, he could be really handsome with new clothes, a different haircut, and those nails cleaned up! She knew Syd did not look only on the outside of a guy, but also on the inside. Howie had turned out to be quite a nice guy, once he accepted Rhonda as Teddy's girlfriend.

They returned to Union Station around 4 p.m. for dinner, again at the Rice Bowl. While they were in line there, Teddy saw Eric, who was eating with a bunch of deaf friends from campus.

"Rhon..." Teddy nudged her and discreetly pointed to Eric. "Remember the guy who was punched by the cop on Monday? That's him over there. HEY!" Teddy waved at Eric's direction. "What's the scoop today?"

Eric was minding his own business, sharing news about the Jordan press conference, when he noticed hands waving in the air in his direction. His jaw was still smarting from the punch he had received from that stupid cop. He was happy, though, that he had not retaliated. He was not a violent guy. Everyone came to him because he was very friendly, personable, and charismatic. When the protest started, he had taken up the leadership role at the MSSD entrance, and that was where the cop incident had occurred.

He achieved some notoriety, and many reporters had clamored for an interview with him as a result. Plus he got many requests from girls for his dorm room number, and that had been a boon to his social standing on campus. Even Kappa Gamma frat members had approached him with the possibilitiy of being offered a rush the following fall semester, as it was too late for the spring. He really had made out good with the protest happening in his backyard.

"Teddy! Did you watch Jordan's announcement? He backed away from the board and Zinser! Now he is behind us all the way. We were so mad at him and now all is forgiven, water under the bridge." His teeth showed as he offered a broad smile at Teddy. Whoa, was that the girl who had offended everyone with her backing of Zinser? He'd better find out. Otherwise, Teddy was setting himself up for trouble. He did not want to jump to conclusions here. Better to err on the side of caution with something like this. He waited for Teddy to come over with his tray.

"Hi, Eric. That is great news. Everyone was expecting that to happen, and I am glad it did. This is Rhonda, my girlfriend." He then quickly added, "She has come around to our side, and contrary to what you may have heard, she is with us now. This is Sydney, her former roommate at Catholic. That's Howie, my best friend!"

Eric felt a huge sense of relief. So she did come around after all. Good for Teddy. There were a few chairs empty, so he motioned for them to sit with the others at the table. Gratefully, Teddy sat down and had Rhonda sit next to him. Howie sat a few chairs away with Sydney. They were very hungry and ate quickly so they could catch up on the news once they finished. Eric could see they had not eaten for a while. Maybe they had been in DC like tourists, off campus.

There was a TV broadcasting the news and suddenly a breaking news alert blared from the screen. Rhonda's head jerked up and she dropped her fork into the bowl. She could not believe it. Her eyes turned to Teddy and she signed, "Zinser is resigning! Lemme interpret for all you guys!"

Everyone else stopped eating and stared at Rhonda. They had not realized she was hearing, because of her sign fluency. Plus, they had caught what she signed to Teddy about Zinser.

"This is at the J.W. Marriott Hotel here in DC, guys. Zinser just said she resigned. She wanted to restore order and allow Gallaudet to return to its ordinary business of education as it had been for the past 124 years. She also admitted she had not realized how monumental this entire movement was. Now that she knows and understands, she is stepping out of the picture! Yahoo!"

Everyone cheered and clinked their sodas. Teddy admired Zinser for being open to resigning. There was Spilman alongside her, looking sad, like an abandoned puppy. What a different picture from that day when everyone had walked out of the gymnasium at the insistence of Harvey Goodstein! His eyes stayed riveted to the TV and he saw something that really blew his mind.

"HEY! Guys, look at this, I love it!" He pointed up at the screen. Everyone stared. It was a widescreen shot of two headstones on the street. One said "IN MEMORY OF JEAN BASSET-SPILMAN" and the other said "IN MEMORY OF DR. ZINSER." Both were dated March 10th, 1988. The headstones were obviously placed on the street, judging from the crosswalk that was right near Spilman's headstone. There was a tarp covering the area right in front of the two headstones. Warning tripod lights blinked yellow as if to call attention to them. It was a surreal picture and so apropos. It had been such a providential coincidence that street crews had been doing repairs on roads near Gallaudet, especially the one right in front of the security booth!

There was a huge celebration at the Field House that night. Teddy, Howie, Rhonda, and Sydney found themselves seated on the floor surrounded by hundreds of screaming people. To Rhonda and Syd, this was similar to being at a rock concert like the one they had gone to only last semester. They had to do a double-take before realizing that this was a university of the deaf. Syd had not expected so much noise to come from these students' mouths, as they signed without voicing. Rhonda had warned her on their walk back from dinner at Union Station that it would be very loud when they got there. She had not believed her and now wished she had brought earplugs to drown out the noise, which was deafening.

They watched with swelled hearts as speaker after speaker went onto the stage and spurred the crowd on. Greg Hlibok provoked the loudest and most demonstrative display anyone had ever seen. Someone ran onto the stage and placed an armband on his right sleeve to show solidarity with the protest. Greg was very tired from all the activity that week, but he was running on adrenaline. Imagine meeting Ted Koppel, Marlee Matlin, politicians, even celebrities all week!

Teddy wished he had the same leadership skills as Greg. They had even met recently during a cafeteria panel discussion on mainstreaming versus schools for the deaf. He could vividly remember walking onto the stage and Greg stepping toward him with an outstretched hand.

He had been impressed by how friendly and welcoming Greg was, knowing that he, Teddy, was considered to be on the fringe looking in because of his upbringing as a mainstreamed, oral deaf student in a hearing family while Greg was seen as being among the "cream of the crop" with a deaf family, residential school background, and YLC camp experience. Teddy wished him nothing but the best and he had watched him become even more prominent during the protest week.

Rhonda couldn't believe how loud it was. Syd next to her was puzzled because she kept hearing, "FOUR! FOUR! FOUR!" and wondered what that meant, so she leaned to her left, and her left shoulder bumped Rhonda on her right side.

"Rhon, what are they yelling? Can you tell me? I keep hearing them yell the same thing over and over." Syd had become really fascinated with this protest and was immersed in the speeches that had just taken place, with Rhonda voice interpreting. She really wanted to learn this visual-oriented language. Howie, on her right, was fast becoming a dating prospect. What better way to become fluent in ASL than date a deaf guy? She was going to ask him to get coffee maybe tonight, definitely tomorrow.

"Oh, the number four represents the four demands that the protest sent the board: fire Zinser and pick a deaf president, fire Spilman, make the board more than fifty percent deaf, and no reprisals for the entire week. That's basically what they are saying. Now with Zinser out, they have three more demands left before the protest ends."

Ahhh. She had read something about that in the paper. That made perfect sense. The momentum definitely was on their side so she didn't blame them for not stopping until they got what they wanted. Judging from the energy emanating from this crowd, she knew it would happen in a matter of days. There was no way the board could maintain the status quo with Zinser resigning and Jordan withdrawing his support of her selection. If the board members were stubborn enough, then chaos would reign on this previously tranquil campus. Rhonda had described Gallaudet to her in the past as an oasis where everyone was happy and friendly.

When the meeting ended, Syd nudged Rhonda again and asked her how to sign "You, me, coffee tonight?" After watching her a few times, she got up on her feet and turned to her right to face Howie. Better get this over with or she would chicken out! Howie did look intimidating, as he was taller than she was, but she knew he wouldn't bite, figuratively or literally.

She tapped him on the shoulder. He turned to face her, an expectant look on his face. His eyes opened wide as she signed, "COFFEE YOU ME TONIGHT?" His face broke into one of the biggest smiles she had ever seen and he nodded slowly. Their eyes locked and he put his left arm around her. She felt really cozy nestling up against him. He was such a nice guy, and she had seen that ever since they met out in front of Gallaudet's Fowler Hall the other day. She had been so scared when she came to the campus from her dorm looking for Teddy.

Off they went to walk to Union Station. Teddy stood there, mouth open. He looked at Rhonda questioningly and she told him Syd had asked Howie out for coffee. He laughed and shook his head.

"What have you done, babe? First me, now Howie...deaf guy with hearing gal! This is way too much!"

A sudden thought entered Teddy's mind. Spring break! What were they gonna do about that? It was sure to be on everyone's mind after tonight if the protest did not end tomorrow as expected. Was Spilman going to be that stubborn, along with the rest of the board? After what he'd seen all week, anything was possible!

"Rhon, I just thought of something. What are you doing next week? I was going to head out to Long Island, but if this doesn't end by Sunday, I am staying right here to continue the fight."

He could see several conversations around him centering on the same topic as the one they were discussing. It was sure to be discussed at tomorrow night's meeting in Field House. There also was to be a huge march on the Capitol. Howie and Sydney had told them to meet at the front gate of Gallaudet at 10:00 when they would be starting the march through DC from campus. Somehow they would find each other.

Chapter Six:
Friday, March 11th, 1988

The following morning was full of activity. Even before 9:00, there were hundreds of people milling about in front of Fowler Hall. There was not a single cloud in the sky. The temperature was a balmy sixty-five degrees and it was as if God himself had arranged for the most perfect weather setting possible. Many people commented in the crowd as they greeted each other that they definitely had His endorsement! Teddy had laughed when he saw that, and he mentioned it to Rhonda, who smiled.

There were approximately ten people right near the security booth, holding onto a very long banner that proclaimed: "WE STILL HAVE A DREAM." Teddy wondered who these individuals were and how they had gotten this banner for today. As a history buff and social studies major, he was familiar with this particular banner.

He told Rhonda that it came from the Crispus Attucks Museum based in Washington, DC. Supporters of the Martin Luther King birthday had hoisted it during their march efforts to establish MLK's birth as a national holiday. Rhonda was impressed yet again at Teddy's encyclopedic knowledge. It was one of the many great qualities she was attracted to.

Teddy couldn't believe the variety in this crowd that was gathering here. There were some NTID students from Rochester, New York -- approximately fifty. People of all ages were here, ready to show their support of DPN. Even some mothers with baby carriages were lounging about. One dog had a small cloth banner that made him laugh out loud: "MY DOG KNOWS MORE SIGNS THAN SPILMAN!"

He nudged Rhonda and pointed to the dog. Priceless! Was there any end to people's creativity? Other people were carrying a huge placard saying: "BOARD BUSTERS," referring to one of the demands which asked for a fifty-one percent deaf majority on the board with Spilman's resignation.

People kept coming and coming. By 10:00, the numbers were so massive that he had never seen anything like it before. Finally, the people up front with the MLK banner started walking. There were cops standing on Florida Avenue to stop all traffic. People in their cars were staring at the protestors and some of them flashed "ILY" signs to them, having learned that from the media's coverage all week. Students saw that and they kept walking, filled with purpose. It took fifteen minutes for everyone to exit the front entrance of the campus before traffic was allowed to resume.

Rhonda could hear all of the honking and cheering along their route. She told Teddy it was incredibly loud. As he could not hear very much, she described how many cars were honking as they walked by, along with yelling and screaming, especially on the busy streets where the governmental offices were. Windows were open and throngs of people had peered out to watch this memorable occasion.

Marchers were grouped by state. Teddy could see the signs with each state on them. There was a dark brown placard with MINNE-SOTA in yellow letters, easily visible for anyone to see. It was harder to see the other states' names, but people managed to find their home state and join the group marching under that banner. It was a stroke of genius! He wondered who had thought of it.

There was Tom marching with Bridget! They were too far away for him to get their attention, but he laughed at what Tom was wearing. That was Tom, no doubt about it. He was draped in an American flag with a yellow Gallaudet hat on. Bridget had her Gallaudet sweatshirt on. They were alone and obviously enjoying this experience.

It was just as well. Teddy felt lucky that he had found Rhonda after Bridget decided that Tom was a better match for her. He felt bad about the cafeteria milk incident. It had happened just a few days before the protest happened. At dinner, he had turned around to talk to someone behind him and when he turned back to the table, he saw shrimp soaking in his glass of milk. He had somehow lost his temper and thrown the glass at Tom, thinking it was he who had done it. The milk drenched Bridget who was sitting on his left. She had never forgiven him for that and she decided to date Tom instead of him. It was a lesson for Teddy: always stay calm!

Continuing to walk on the streets of DC, he saw one student with a great sign: "TO BOARD OF TRUSTEES: Don't Tread on Gallaudet" with a snake that was poised to attack. That was an obvious reference to the famous slogan from the American Revolution when the colonists resisted Great Britain's efforts to squash protests for independence. That was very creative. Who was holding that sign? Luis?! Good for him! Obviously, he was incorporating what he had learned in class!

It took over two hours for all of the protestors to arrive at the Capitol and get settled. The four leaders took their place on top of the steps in front of the Rotunda. Greg Hlibok was dressed the most formally of the four, in a grey jacket and black slacks. Jerry Covell had his trademark denim jacket and jeans on. Bridgetta Bourne wore a Gallaudet grey sweatshirt and white pants. Tim Rarus stood behind the other three, clapping and cheering on the crowd for their efforts the entire week. He had jeans on also, plus a Levi's blue dress shirt.

The crowd went wild at the sight of the leaders. Every time the four applauded the crowd, they got the same adulation back from them. It was an emotionally charged moment. They had worked very hard to arrive at this point. Then, speaker after speaker came forth to orate to the students. Some were hearing, others deaf. Congressman Steve Gunderson lauded the students for their brave stand. Then, the crowd went wild when Robert Silverstein, who ran the US Senate Subcommittee on the Handicapped, shook Greg's hand, paying homage to DPN's four demands.

The speeches ended and people still stood there, awed by what they had witnessed. Teddy and Rhonda decided to walk off to the mall again like they had the other day. After all, they needed their alone time to rebuild the connection they had almost lost early that week. Hand in hand, they strolled to the reflecting pool. Teddy saw an empty bench and asked Rhonda if she wanted to sit down after standing for several hours straight. She agreed, and it felt so good to rest again.

"Babe..." Teddy started to say. His throat suddenly had a lump and he faltered. His emotions were so charged right now for this woman who had touched his heart after lowering his emotional walls and defenses. She had soothed his pain and made him feel whole again. For that, he would spend the rest of his life repaying the favor.

"Thank you for coming back and finding me. I was so afraid of losing you." His eyes became watery. It had nothing to do with the wind, nor any dust that came from the ground. He was crying out of happiness that he had found his second half. Rhonda could see how overwhelmed he felt and she inched closer to him on the bench, putting her arms around him. She would never let go of Teddy, ever. He had touched her heart in a place that nobody had touched before.

They embraced, words not needed at the moment. The connection had been repaired and they were back on the road to being together. As if by unspoken command, they stood up and started walking back to Gallaudet. Each was deep in thought, happy at the prospect of many happy memories ahead of them. But the protest itself was not over, so they needed to focus on that. Spring break would have to wait.

Chapter Seven
Saturday, March 12th, 1988

The next day was a much more restful one after the hectic week they had just lived through. There was a huge cookout in front of Fowler Hall where students served Spilmandogs and Board Burgers throughout the afternoon. The board was inundated with thousands of telegrams, letters, and phone calls, with ninety-nine percent running in favor of the students' three remaining demands. Some of the board members were starting to rethink their position on who to pick for president.

There was a huge table at Fowler with all of the news articles of the day referring to DPN. People lined up to read each one and keep abreast of what was happening. Everyone was holding their breath to see what the board would do next. Would they finally capitulate and do the right thing, or prolong the struggle that was playing itself out for the entire world to see? Nobody dared to imagine the anger and resentment if the weekend went by with no concessions from the board on the three remaining demands.

Teddy could only see more protests and acting out by students during spring break. He vowed to stay on campus if Monday came and there was still the status quo of paternalism and oppression by Spilman and her fellow board members. Rhonda said she would stay also for the duration. If the protest ended over the weekend, they had alternate plans to maybe visit Long Island to see her parents and his.

The sun set on the Gallaudet campus with no news from the Mayflower Hotel. Everyone was walking on eggshells and it was frustrating to see that there had been no progress in the talks between the student leaders and the board. Finally, in the early evening, word spread that Greg Hlibok had left the conference room where the board was meeting. When people asked him what was going on, he just shook his head and said he did not know anything.

Chapter Eight

Sunday, March 13th, 1988

Sunday morning and afternoon slowly went by. Still no news. Teddy and Rhonda spent the day together in her room with Howie and Syd. They ordered out for pizza at dinner instead of going to the cafeteria, which was mobbed with students waiting and watching the TV sets for any tidbit of news. Teddy had a hunch this was a big moment about to happen, so he asked the other three to walk over to Ole Jim where people were standing outside in the cool breeze. He knew that the organizers of the protest were there waiting for the news, if it did come.

They left Rhonda's dorm and walked across campus. They could see that others were making the same trek as if there was something pulling all of them to the same place at the same time. Teddy knew then that his hunch just might have been right on the money. Luckily, the weather was cooperating like it had all week. He put his right hand into Rhonda's left and squeezed it lightly. It felt so nice sharing his days and nights with a woman who appreciated him for who he was: a Deaf man fluent in ASL and immersed in the Deaf world.

All of a sudden, people started running past them. What was going on? Something had happened. He jerked Rhonda's arm and said, "Let's go! I think the news finally arrived!" So, they started picking up their pace and ran across campus, past the library, past the Edward Miner Gallaudet Building. There was a huge throng already there with arms and fists pumping in the air. They had done it! There were many happy facial expressions. Some were even weeping openly. He could see many prominent deaf faces hugging people left and right, even those they had never met before.

Luis! He could see his roommate only a few feet away and he wanted to get the news of what was happening. He beckoned toward Luis and told Rhonda he was going to find out what was happening. Rhonda walked with him over to Luis.

"Hey, roomie! You remember Rhonda?" Luis looked at her and nodded, his teeth showing with a smile that nobody had ever seen on his face before. He felt so ecstatic and had to tell Teddy.

"I remember you, yes! Good to see you all here. Guess what? Phil Bravin just called from the Embassy Hotel with the news! He told Greg that the board has given in to all four demands officially!"

Teddy screamed and turned around to Rhonda. His eyes opened up like Niagara Falls and he hugged her tightly, lifting her off the ground and twirling her around. Rhonda giggled and held on to him. She was so thrilled for Gallaudet and for Teddy. Howie and Syd held hands and cheered.

"There's more! Did you know that Phil would not tell anyone other than Greg? He even asked Greg who his siblings were to make sure it was really him! Plus Phil himself is the new chair of the board and there will be a deaf majority very soon! They had a long TTY conversation and Phil assured Greg that the board had officially given in to DPN! Right now, on TV, Phil is making the same press announcement. Everyone is celebrating!"

It turned out that Spilman resigned, calling herself an "obstacle" and telling everyone that she was removing herself as one. That had been such an apt description of her in the eyes of many protestors. Teddy felt very confident in the future of Gallaudet and he hoped that a lesson had been learned from this whole movement. Where else in the world could people feel free to express themselves so openly and take over a university like in the sixties and seventies? He felt fortunate to be living in such a country.

Luis gestured excitedly at him. It turned out that Jordan was coming to the Abbey where Teddy had sat down with Howie and chatted with Mimi and her boyfriend early that week. The world had done a 180-degree turn. He had been estranged from Rhonda then and his world had turned upside down that day. Plus he had been feeling so rejected and isolated with his family not signing, plus losing his dream woman in one fell swoop.

Now he had everything back in spades. It reminded him of the Book of Job. As he recalled from religious school, Job had lost his wives, kids, livestock, everything as a test of his faith in God. Eventually, Satan had been unable to shake his rock-hard faith, so God rewarded him with even more blessings.

Finally, he was able to stop crying. Were people actually capable of crying endlessly? Or did the body produce only so much and then shut down production? He felt as if he had exhausted all of the tears that his body had made. There just was no more coming out of his eyes. He rubbed them to get rid of the blurriness. He wanted to feast his eyes on Rhonda and share this moment with her. They hugged again tightly. A few minutes later, people started to walk to the Abbey. Teddy did not feel like he had enough strength to keep celebrating. His body was starting to feel the effects of the entire week.

"Rhon, would it be OK if we just sat outside the Ely Center and watched everyone celebrate? There's a bench we can sit on to share the excitement in the air with people we know."

Rhonda nodded and said, "Sure, honey. We can definitely do that. It is so nice out here, and not crowded like it would be inside." She voiced for Syd what they had talked about. The four of them walked across the road past the EMG Building toward the Ely Center. There were some benches that were not taken, so they went ahead to sit down. Howie looked at Sydney and marveled at the fact that she had learned so much in just one day with him. She was a natural! Fear was not in her vocabulary. She kept asking for more and more signs, insatiable for them. He had happily obliged and she even used her facial expressions, which was something that most hearing ASL students struggled with.

Howie could see how Syd modeled her facial expressions after watching him and the others use theirs with certain phrases and signs. For example, with yes-no questions, the eyebrows were raised and for wh-questions, they were furrowed. As deaf people could not hear the voice intonation change when a person made a statement or a question, it was vital for a signer to use his or her face to signal the change. Syd had grasped this idea very quickly and was already attempting to do so with Howie's help.

Plus, he knew that Syd would have to learn non-manual markers. A good example he would teach her pertained to size of an object. If it was huge, his mouth would mouth "CHA!" when he signed. For a medium-sized object, he would show her "mmm" with pursed lips. For a small thing, he used "ooo" with his lips slightly open in a round shape. There was so much to show her. Rhonda would definitely help out because she was already adept with NMMs in the short time that she had been at Gallaudet. He also had helped Teddy become more fluent in ASL and he was proud of that.

Howie was curious about Ole Jim, and he leaned forward to look at Teddy. "Did you ever know what Ole Jim was used for when Gallaudet was pretty much brand new?" Surely, Teddy would know the answer, as he was always reading about this campus and its history. He had learned a lot from Teddy in the past month or two with the amount of time they spent together.

Teddy thought for a minute, pulling out the information he had gleaned from his library research. Ole Jim was such an interesting place, the way it had been used prior to its current GUAA office space.

He cleared his throat and asked Rhonda to interpret for Sydney. He did not feel comfortable with SimCom, voicing and signing at the same time. He knew that some people did that, including King Jordan. It was funny how he was unable to understand Jordan when he signed. Due to the fact that Jordan spoke and signed, there was ambiguity in the message that was conveyed. Teddy had to watch the ASL interpreters every time Jordan spoke. This could prove to be a problem down the road with Jordan becoming president of Gallaudet.

Teddy felt that it took away the true meaning of what he wanted to say if he had to do both ASL and speech at the same time. He had learned in his class with Dr. Gerilee Gustason, the deaf woman who came up with Signed Exact English II (SEE II), that the amount of information a teacher was able to convey to a student was halved when SimCom was used instead of voice-off signing. It was ironically better to just voice without signing in terms of the speed of information. No wonder he had learned that much more when he was mainstreamed in public schools from second grade to high school graduation.

"Ole Jim was built in 1881 originally as a gymnasium with an indoor swimming pool, basketball court, and bowling alley. Funding efforts were led by David and Pauline Peikoff in 1978 and the alumni office moved into the renovated space, which used to host athletic events. Maybe one day they will rename Ole Jim after the Peikoffs for their tremendous efforts with fundraising, but that remains to be seen. Renovations were completed in 1982 so GUAA has had its headquarters here since. I've been in there and there are banners all over the walls inside. Gorgeous place!"

Rhonda, Howie, and Sydney watched him, transfixed. They were in awe of Teddy's remembering so much detail of Gallaudet's history. A few minutes went by and nobody said a word. Then, Rhonda said, "Wow! I had no idea. Thanks, babe." She smiled at him and put her arms around him.

Teddy hugged her back. A sudden thought entered his mind. What would happen to the president's house now that it would be the residence of a deaf person? Jordan did have a hearing wife, Linda, and two hearing children. But the fact remained that modifications would be needed to make it accessible for him. He had an idea for a game.

He waved his hand at his three friends. "I wonder what will happen to House One. That's the name we have for the president's house here on campus." He turned his head and pointed to an area opposite College Hall. "The house is right there, across the softball field, behind those office buildings. Those three or four houses there used to be called Faculty Row. They were residences for professors who lived on campus at night. Now...I am curious what they will need to do to accommodate Jordan living there with his family?"

Responses were not long in coming from them. Flashing lights for both the doorbell and fire alarm. TTYs in the bedroom, kitchen, living room, dining room. A television with a caption decoder on top of it. Moving furniture around to make it more deaf-friendly. Change of lighting to reduce the glare and go easy on the eyes.

It would be amazing to watch if they were able to, but Teddy knew very few students had been given the privilege of entering House One. He remembered his trip to the White House just after he had arrived on campus in January. It was a cold, wintry day on a Saturday morning. He went with Tom, Bridget, and another student named Mayra, who was about forty years old. He chuckled at the memory.

"Teddy, what are you laughing about now?" Rhonda noticed his smile and wanted to know what he was thinking about. Teddy went on to tell them the story.

"I went to visit the White House with three other students, Tom, Bridget, and Mayra. Now, Mayra was forty, Tom and Bridget twenty-two. I was twenty-four, like I am now. An old couple in front of us looked at me and said, 'You two have beautiful kids with you.' I had never felt so embarrassed in my life. Mayra told them we were all friends and the couple profusely apologized when they found out our ages!"

All of them laughed out loud. That was funny! The four of them continued to sit there and enjoy their time together, finally being able to relax after such an arduous week emotionally and physically. They got word that there would be a press conference early Monday morning, the 14th, at Ely Center. They wanted to be able to watch it on TV, so they made sure they would be at breakfast before there was a long line snaking around the dorm common area outside. That was where Teddy had been just the past Monday morning talking to friends about Sunday night.

At this press conference, with Teddy, Rhonda, Howie, and Sydney watching the cafeteria TV, King Jordan uttered his most famous quote: "Deaf people can do anything hearing people can -- except hear." He felt the whole place erupt in cheers and yelling. Someone almost upset their breakfast table in the excitement. That quote seemed to resonate within Teddy. He looked at Rhonda and then the new couple, Howie and Syd. They all knew that would be a memorable quote for years to come.

Suddenly, everyone sitting down rushed to the huge window in the far room. What was this? *Never a dull moment on campus*, Teddy mused. He rushed to the window and gaped at what he saw. A small biplane was flying over the Capitol with a banner in red letters: "GALLAUDET – THE WORLD SALUTES YOU!" That could only be Ken Glickman, a deaf pilot. Who had paid for this? What a great gesture by someone to commemorate the protest's success! The four of them stood there watching the plane circle the area for everyone to see.

Chapter Nine

Aftermath

The following week after that historic Sunday, the campus slowly returned to its normal routine. The donated trailer home that had served as the headquarters for the DPN Info Center was driven away by the deaf couple that donated its use to the protestors. All of the litter on the ground was cleaned up by students donating their spring vacation time, as they had already canceled plane tickets and hotel reservations.

The campus took on an eerie silence, and it felt deserted with all of the news vans gone. Maintenance crews worked on the lawn, which had been trampled by thousands of feet during the tumultuous week. Moving vans parked at House One so that the new furniture could be brought in. Crews from an electronics company came to install the lighting system that Teddy and his friends discussed, as a deaf person needed that in his or her home for the doorbell, fire alarm, and other reasons.

Teddy woke up on Monday morning in his dorm room. Had the previous week actually happened? He shook his head violently and rubbed his eyes. It was funny how he could not see very well at all, so whenever he woke up, everything was blurry. Since he was eight years old and bought his first pair of glasses, he had always been near-sighted and needed those glasses to be able to see. He remembered his extreme fear of turning blind. That was why he had been afraid of the dark as long as he could remember, and he did not overcome that fear until he was seventeen.

He had gone to a friend's house in Little Neck and he could vividly recall the details of the scariest moment of his life. He and Sean had gotten into the twin beds in Sean's room, as his older brother was off to college, then Sean's father came in and said good night. Then, he flicked the lights off, turning the room into pitch blackness.

Teddy had almost panicked due to his phobia, and he willed himself to breathe slowly and not break down. He was a senior in high school! So, his hands gripped the thin blanket that was draped over him. Eventually, his breath slowed and he forced his eyes to close. Before he knew it, morning had arrived with Sean nudging him awake. He had done it! From that day forward, his phobia had improved dramatically.

Why had he been so afraid of the dark? He could trace it back to the *Little House on the Prairie* episode where Mary Ingalls woke up one morning completely blind. He could not remember what the cause was, but it had unnerved him completely to the point where he could imagine that happening to him. Laura Ingalls Wilder, who wrote the series of novels about her family in the Midwest during the 1800s, had woken up next to Mary, bewildered at her sister's screaming.

Pa and Ma came running up the stairs to see what the heck was going on. Mary kept screaming, "I am blind! I can't see!" From that day forward, Teddy had required some kind of nightlight anywhere in a room he slept in so that when he opened his eyes, he could make sure he was not blind.

Getting out of bed, he vowed to walk over to Rhonda's room. She had, for hours last night, talked to different people to apologize for her instrangience against the protest and supporting the board. Everyone had been accepting of what she said to them, much to her relief. Teddy was with her, standing off a respectful distance with Howie and Sydney. He had interpreted for Syd in a low voice so she would understand what was basically going on.

The party had gone on until 3 a.m. all over campus. Even Jordan's two teenagers had stayed out with the deaf students to celebrate. Imagine, the president of the university letting his kids stay out that late. He knew it was a once-in-a-lifetime opportunity that would never happen again so he showed remarkable leniency. The two teens had been elated, and after being warned not to even think about consuming alcohol, they were let loose to adoring crowds who served as hundreds of babysitters for free. Jordan knew they would be safer on campus than anywhere else except House One.

After showering and dressing, Teddy strolled over to Clerc Hall. Taking the elevator to the fourth floor, he came up to her door and knocked. Then, he rang the bell just in case she did not hear the knocks. This was where their relationship had been saved, with her note in that envelope taped to the door. It had been a turning point for his feelings about her and started them on the road to being together again, this time as a couple as well as friends.

The door opened and there she was, all dressed and ready to go. Her face lit up as she saw Teddy standing there. How good it felt to have him back in her life as more than just a good friend! Her thoughts drifted to the drive she had made from DC to Long Island. Every mile had felt like a piece of her was being ripped off like Velcro. It was the most painful drive of her life. How had she made it home safely? She could barely see the road through her tears. On top of that, it had not been good weather, with some rain and fog. That was all in the past now as she looked forward to a future with him.

"Hi, there!" She wanted to make sure he knew how happy she was to see him. A promise she had made to herself -- never take him for granted ever again. She had even called Syd early this morning. Howie spent the night at her dorm room with them talking the night away. She was learning so much ASL, and luckily she had a sponge for a mind, so she retained pretty much all of it. Syd was very motivated and was going to apply as a special undergraduate student for the fall semester of 1988. It would be fun to have a friend to visit on campus when she went back to Catholic. She could always stay with Syd and visit Teddy.

Teddy smiled at seeing her in person. He wondered if she would ask him to go to Long Island to meet both her parents and his. Now that would prove to be interesting. At breakfast, she did bring up the topic of visiting both sets of parents and he was hesitant about it due to communication issues for both hers and his, in different ways. She was insistent and really wanted him to come along with her.

He relented after a few hours that morning, as she usually could persuade him to do something he did not want to do. She had that effect on him. He would always shake his head at her, chuckling to himself. She punched him playfully on the arm whenever she saw him do that at her. It was a private communication that nobody else knew about.

When they got back to her dorm room, she told him to sit on her bed and watch as she dialed her parents' number on the phone. He consented and she waited for the line to ring. Finally, someone answered.

"Hi! It's Rhonda…who's this?" She signed to Teddy as she spoke and she would proceed to sign what her mom or dad said as well, for his benefit.

"It's Dad. We are so proud of you guys!" He was happy to hear from her. Her voice was lighthearted, so that was a good sign. As long as she was happy and Teddy treated her with love and respect, he would accept the fact that her boyfriend was deaf. He did regret the way he had addressed the whole issue, and his wife had been angry with him all week because of it. After reading the two books that he took out of Bellerose Library, he had felt quite humbled by how wrong he had been.

"Rhon, I really am sorry about how I reacted to the news that you were dating Teddy. Will you forgive me? Your mom gave me quite a piece of her mind after I had said those terrible things to you!" He sat down at the kitchen table where she had given him a tongue lashing, deservedly so. He heard footsteps coming down the stairs and his wife came into the room. She looked at him questioningly. He covered the mouthpiece and mouthed, "Rhonda from Gallaudet. Teddy with her!"

She squealed and seized the phone out of his hand before he could react. "Rhonda, baby! How are you? I just saw your dad on the phone and he told me it was you. Are you coming back home? With him?" She really hoped her daughter would come visit with Teddy. It was time to meet this extraordinary young man who had such a tremendous impact on their daughter. There was so much to do! She had not finished spring cleaning. It was her favorite ritual of the year, after Christmas. Once all of the decorations had been put away after New Year's, her energies focused on what needed to be done to get the house back in shipshape order.

Kieran had lived through twenty-plus years of her yearly routine. Thanks to her discipline, he had turned into quite the organizer himself. Before meeting her, he had been quite a slob, putting things wherever, and as a consequence he would often forget where a specific object was until he thought about it for a while. Now, he had a structured routine and very rarely had to struggle to remember where everything was. He even conducted his financial affairs the same way, and maintained an extensive filing system. His wife really should be a professional organizer.

With these organizing and filing skills, it had been a piece of cake for him to gather information on deaf culture all weekend after Rhonda returned to DC. His files were already bulging with copies that he had made at the library, spending a minor fortune. He had files with labels such as DEAF HISTORY, DEAF CULTURE, ASL LINGUISTICS, and CURRENT EVENTS.

He was able to organize the ever-growing amount of information he was gathering in order to understand Rhonda's new world that she was sharing with Teddy. He had been relentless, poring over the material several times. He was starting to see the big picture. Deaf people had always been overlooked, oppressed, and underestimated throughout history. He included himself in that infamous group of people and vowed to make up for it from this point on.

He saw Esther's outstretched arm with the receiver in it. Obviously, there was more to talk about. He took it and started listening. Rhonda told him that they were coming that night, arriving around 8 p.m. Great! He would get to meet this young man sooner than he had dared to expect. He had a mission today: review the signs that he had just learned from Rhonda and the books, and read through his deaf history notes. That way, he would be better prepared and more comfortable meeting Teddy even though Rhonda would be there with him to interpret.

Chapter Ten:

Long Island

Teddy and Rhonda packed their bags quickly and they were on the road before rush hour started. They had experience navigating the route between DC and Long Island, so they could figure out the best time(s) to leave, depending on which direction they drove. If they left at 2:00, they would miss the rush out of Baltimore and be in Jersey by 4:30, stop at the first rest area for a while, and get to relax a bit before hitting mid-Jersey during rush hour. It would be a breeze because everyone was exiting New York City by then and it was nothing but country for another couple of hours until they hit the Verrazano Bridge near the city. Hopefully, there would be no jams tonight.

It was a challenge for Teddy to drive with a passenger in the car. Even though deaf people use their peripheral vision much better than hearing drivers, it was hard to focus on Rhonda's side of a conversation even with her fluent ASL skills. When it became dark outside, it was even harder to do the driving. That was why he preferred a hearing person to drive, not him, especially in city environments. If there were few cars on the road, he felt more comfortable turning his eyes off the road for a few seconds.

But for a woman to drive a man, even in today's society, was sort of frowned upon. The man was expected to be the leader and let the woman follow. That was why signs for FATHER, BOY, UNCLE, GRANDFATHER all originated above the nose (upper half of the face) while signs for MOTHER, GIRL, AUNT, GRANDMOTHER used the bottom half below the nose. Some habits die hard. Even though signs had changed to become more politically correct -- like for countries --

the gender-related signs had stayed the same. Would they ever change? Good question.

Teddy marveled at how people had come up with new signs for some racial groups. For instance, CHINA used to be signed with the handshape "C" next to an eye, signifying the slanted eyes commonly found in Asia. Now, the sign was an index finger outlining the warlord shirts from ancient times. The same went for JAPAN with the eye; now people signed it thinking of the islands. The list went on and on.

Teddy forced himself to focus on his driving and try to follow Rhonda's dialogue with him. She was babbling about her parents and how they had acted with guys who she had dated in the past, mostly in high school. She never brought home anyone from college except for Roy. He was already nervous about meeting them and did not need to add more stress to his emotions, which were running wild trying to imagine what her folks would say and do with him there.

Plus, he forgot to ask her about pets! He was deathly allergic to cats and bigger dogs that shed their hair. Golden retrievers and Labradors were the worst breeds for him to be around. He loved those dogs as they were very smart and playful, but to be in the same house as one or two of those dogs? Forget about it. His asthma and allergies definitely would act up in no time due to the dander and shed hair. He really should have asked Rhonda about this before consenting to the visit.

"Excuse me, Rhon…" He forced his eyes to stay on the highway. They were passing that huge white statue of the Virgin Mary, as there was some kind of convent or seminary on the east side of the highway. He always saluted the statue whenever he drove from DC to NY. He could not see it when he drove south, for some reason. He said a silent prayer for God to help him be strong tonight with her folks.

"Do your parents have any pets? I should have asked you before, but in all the excitement, I never did." Teddy awaited her answer with bated breath. If there indeed were any pets in the house that he was allergic to, he had a serious problem. He mentally crossed his fingers (and toes), in anticipation of her reply.

"No, they don't have any pets. Why? Are you allergic to them?" Rhonda was surprised to hear this question from Teddy about pets at her parents' house. Whew. Their cat had just passed away a few months ago after she left for Catholic that September. Obviously, it was broken-hearted at her absence and had not been its usual self ever since. She knew it was terrible to feel relief at a pet's death, but they had practically fumigated the whole house after Felix had been brought to vet and put to sleep. They had sworn never to get a cat again because so many friends and family were allergic, and thus could not visit.

"Yep, deathly allergic to dander. Always have been. Same for all in my family. I had a serious asthma attack once in high school. My friend Vance had a girlfriend whose mom had forty-nine cats! She was called the 'Cat Lady' because of that. Also, I almost had to go to the emergency room a few times due to being at friends' homes who had cats."

Whoa! She hoped her parents had kept up with the house "fumigating." If not, that was a bridge they would have to cross when they came to it. She knew that Mom and Dad were immaculate, especially Mom. Dad had followed her example after they married and moved in together as a couple. She had seen pictures of his "bachelor pad" and the mess had not looked good at all.

Finally, they got to the first rest area in New Jersey and agreed to get off for gas and dinner. They attracted stares in the restaurant while eating because they were not voicing at all. People were not used to seeing deaf people in southern New Jersey, because there was a small population of deaf people, unlike bigger cities like New York City or Baltimore. Even Trenton had many deaf people, or deafies, because of the Marie Katzenbach School for the Deaf which had been there for so long.

Rhonda was getting used to the stares also. She knew Teddy's stories about wearing hearing aids and how they had attracted unwanted attention. She had seen his story about being the first boy in his class to wear a "bra" (as the boys in the locker room had derisively called it) to hold his body hearing aids. He joked that he was like a woman, adept at clasping and unclasping the hook that held the "bra" together.

He had gotten his first behind-the-ear aid when he turned ten. This was a big change for him, a very welcome one. No longer would he be encumbered by this chest contraption that he had worn for so many years. He then let his hair grow a little longer to cover his ears. He was embarrassed by them.

Sometimes, to make matters worse, the aids would emit feedback. Once, during a big test in social studies, students thought there was a UFO landing outside due to the high-frequency hum they were hearing. After a few minutes, everyone realized that Teddy's aids were giving off this noise due to loose earmolds, one or both of them. It was funny because he was the only student who was focused on his test while everyone -- including the teacher -- was unable to concentrate. He was snapped out of his concentration by one student who tapped him and pointed to the teacher.

Rhonda hoped her parents would act normally around Teddy. The worst thing they could do would be to enunciate the words in an exaggerated fashion. Teddy had told her another story (he had a thousand of them based on his experience as a deaf person). When in eighth grade, he had a teacher who was an absolute moron when it came to pronouncing words and common sense. During spelling tests, he would mouth words with such exaggeration that Teddy was unable to understand him at all. He had to tell Mr. Dracken to talk just a little slower than normal. That way, he would understand much more. So, he did, and Teddy started getting 100s on the tests.

His parents realized the class was too easy and petitioned for honors English. That class consisted of the "cream of the crop" with the eventual valedictorian and salutatorian of the class of 1982. Almost every student who would place in the top ten percent of the senior class was in this particular section of English. Teddy had not been happy to be moved into this class. But he realized later that he had been lucky because the expectations were much higher and he was challenged to his maximum capacity by the workload. The teachers in honors English were the best in the school district and the students were very nice to him.

One particular memory had stuck with Teddy when he got a special excerpt from a magazine that talked about literacy. Bill Cosby was featured in the two-page spread in the center of the excerpt with the longest word in his vocabulary that he had learned as a high school student. Teddy had been intrigued by this word and spent two hours memorizing this forty-five-letter word: pneumonoultramicroscopicsilicovolcanoconiosis. It was a lung disease caused by inhaling volcanic ash!

When he first uttered the long word to Rhonda, she fell off the bed laughing so hard that tears ran down her cheeks. It had been the funniest thing to hear him drawl nineteen syllables right out of his mouth like that. It was the last thing she had expected at that moment. It was one of her favorite moments that she often thought about when she was not with him.

Upon finishing dinner, they cleaned up and went back to the car. Rhonda was driving now, so Teddy could afford to sit back and relax a bit. He had been keyed up during the drive from DC to this point and he was done for the night. Having to concentrate at night with the road and their conversation was going to be too much even for a good lipreader like Teddy. The best lipreaders still only got thirty percent of what was on the lips. The rest they had to guess through context clues. Plus, Rhonda would sign and that brought up the percentage to a much higher level. Still, it zapped his energy as he worried about being a safe driver on the highways and streets.

It seemed like a quick trip after they got the gas tank filled up. Why was gas cheaper in New Jersey than New York? Both Teddy and

Rhonda had commented on that and they always did wonder what affected the prices to make them ten to twenty cents cheaper. They did count their blessings that there were no lines at this time of day. Teddy could remember living through the seventies as a kid, riding with his mom and having to wait forever in gas lines at a gas station due to the OPEC boycott of America back then.

At approximately 8:00 p.m., they finally saw the Verrazano Bridge. All of a sudden, the imminent meeting with her parents became real to Teddy. He started to sweat and fidget in his seat. Rhonda noticed this and she put her right hand on top of his leg.

"It will be all right. Don't worry! My parents will love you. Guess what they did before I came back to DC?"

"No idea. What did they do?"

"They went to the library with me and got some books on deaf culture plus ASL. My dad is very determined to communicate with you. I taught them some phrases and words while I was home with them." Rhonda was proud of the fact that her parents had opened their minds about Teddy. They only wanted her happy with whomever she dated.

Teddy stared at her, mouth forming an "ooh." He was impressed. Did his parents ever do that? No! Her folks hadn't even met him yet, but they were putting in the effort just for him, and for her too. He vowed to give them a chance when they arrived. Plus there was no cat to worry about! That was a big plus. He hoped they were truly nice and genuine people like his parents were. He just wished his mom and dad would be willing to learn ASL for him and his deaf friends. He secretly wished his sisters would somehow have a deaf child so he would have deaf relatives. Rhonda was a dream come true for him, a woman who signed fluently. Howie was going to have the same thing once Sydney picked up her signing vocabulary in a short time.

As the sign for New Hyde Park Road inched closer by the minute, there was no traffic at all. There was a slight drizzle falling, but nothing to worry about. Finally, they arrived at her parents' house at approximately 9:00 p.m. Pulling into the driveway, Rhonda parked the car right behind her mother's BMW. She knew that her dad sometimes had to go to work late for emergencies or very early in the morning. So she always parked behind Mom's car to allow him to get out of the driveway without having to move another car.

Teddy opened his car door and got out, stretching his legs. It had been a long ride, but had gone by quickly. Looking at the Jennings' house, he liked it right away. It reminded him of the Waltons' white Colonial house, with a porch that went around the front and side. It looked brand-new, but he knew it was about forty years old. That whole neighborhood was from the forties after the suburbs exploded in terms of population after the second World War.

This was it! They took their bags and walked up the driveway. There was a brick walkway that curved to the left, ending at the front door. Before either of them could ring the doorbell, the front door opened. There they were, his arm around her shoulders.

"Come right in, guys! Hi, Tinkerbell. Been so long since we saw you!" He chuckled and wrapped his arms around her. His baby girl was home again, for the second time that week. He liked it this way and even though he wouldn't admit it, he missed her more than anything.

There was Teddy. He looked presentable enough, but he did seem nervous. He remembered the first time he had met Esther's parents, Jacob and Deidre Bunning. He had been so nervous he almost peed in his pants. Mr. Bunning had been a career military veteran, so he was an imposing figure for anyone. Any suitor that Esther brought home had to endure an interrogation session in the study with Mr. Bunning. End of story. No negotiation about it.

So, he had gone into the study and survived a thirty-minute question and answer session with Esther's father. Obviously, he had said the right things because when they came out, the father had walked over to Esther. He put his arm around her, looked down at her face, and smiled, nodding. That had been the moment when Kieran knew everything was going to be OK. He had then promised himself he would never put his future son-in-law through that kind of ordeal, let alone a deaf one he was not able to communicate with!

Remembering the deaf culture information he had just learned, he made sure the lighting was adequate for communication, and then noticed the two bags that Rhonda and Teddy had brought into the house. He took them into the dining room and put them in the corner for later. He couldn't wait to show Teddy what he had learned in such a short time.

Coming back, he found that they had gone into the kitchen. How funny was that? He remembered that deaf people flocked to the kitchen for some reason. He walked in there and saw Rhonda voicing for Teddy who was signing. He couldn't help but notice that Teddy and Rhonda were not standing together. Why was that?

Then he realized it was easier for him to see her if she was next to her mom, like an interpreter would do in a formal setting such as a classroom or a meeting. It was a good thing he had brushed up on his deaf culture reading. Otherwise, he would have said something really stupid again and drawn his wife's ire as well as Rhonda's!

"It is nice to finally meet you, Mrs. Jennings. Ah, the same for you, Mr. Jennings. I just wanted to thank you for allowing me to stay here with Rhonda. She is terrific!" Teddy looked at them and then at Rhonda, who was finishing her voice interpretation.

Kieran shook Teddy's hand and liked the fact that his grip was firm. He hated it when young men who came to the house to pick up his daughter had the handshake of a dead fish. This was an auspicious beginning for this deaf young man! He cleared his throat, wanting to start things off on the right foot.

"You can call us Kieran and Esther, first name basis. I read that deaf people give sign names to hearing people that they meet, so is it possible for you to give us a sign name? That way, you won't have to fingerspell our names every time."

Teddy had so many thoughts rush through his mind. He was surprised to hear Kieran say such a thing. Obviously, he had done his
homework before meeting him. That was really impressive! He felt
relieved that her parents had taken his visit seriously. He had been
skeptical of their motives, but he was already starting to see a genuinely positive attitude on their part in just a few minutes. He had been
curious whether Kieran would say anything about him and Rhonda not
standing together, but he had not commented on it. That, plus the sign
name request, really was the icing on the cake.

Hmm. What sign name to give her parents? For deaf people, sign
names were significant because each person had his or her own physical
or personal characteristics that stood out for everyone to see. Sometimes a sign name was positive, other times negative. For example, for
Teddy, he had a mole on the right side of his mouth, so his sign name
was a "T" touching that mole. Rhonda's sign name reflected her long,
wavy hair, so he gave her one with "R" sliding from her temple to
shoulder. He did not want to offend her parents within five minutes of
meeting them. This was going to be tricky.

He noticed that Esther wore many bracelets, so he had an idea.
He explained to the three of them that her sign name would be "E"
resting on her wrist. Esther seemed to really like it as she perked up
and smiled broadly. Whew, that was one out of two. Success! Rhonda
beamed at him, proud of his quick thinking. Now on to her dad. There
were no obvious physical characteristics to base the sign name on, so it
was going to be something that stemmed from one of his interests.

"Kieran, can you tell me some of your hobbies? What do you do
in your free time?" It was important to get this information, because a
sign name reflected a person's inner personality if there were no outside mannerisms or physical attributes to look at.

"Good question -- let me think. I am a news aficionado..." He
noticed Rhonda thinking for a minute. Obviously that word "aficio-

nado" was a complex word, so he noticed she fingerspelled it slowly then Teddy nodded his comprehension. Wow, Teddy must have quite a vocabulary! He had purposely put that word in there to gauge this deaf man's verbal skills. Satisfied, he continued to speak.

"I follow the news religiously with politics, religion, current events…" He noticed Teddy's hands moving and his fingers curling and uncurling. Definitely he was going to come up with something pretty quickly, so Kieran stopped talking and waited. Sure enough, Teddy's eyes opened wide and he smiled at Kieran.

"I got it. Put your hand in the shape of 'K' and rest it against your temple. That is modeled after the sign for government…" He showed them the sign for that. "It also is like the sign for politics and republic." Very simple! This was a sign name that was neutral and showed everyone that Kieran was very much into politics and what was happening in the world.

"Thank you, Teddy! I like that. Rhonda, this is a remarkable young man you have brought home with you. I am glad we had the chance to meet him. It is a real pleasure to have you here!" His eyes beamed at Teddy and he just walked over to shake his hand again. This young man was a keeper, that was for sure.

The rest of the two-day visit went smoothly. They went out to eat three times a day and had the best time of their lives. It came as a welcome surprise to Kieran how much Teddy knew about conspiracy theories, Area 51, Roswell, Majestic Twelve, JFK, and other major topics that were of interest to both of them. When Rhonda told them about Teddy reading Erich von Daniken at age eight, he had laughed really hard and loved it! Here was a man after his own heart, intellectually curious and open-minded. Then, they had heard about Teddy's religious journey, starting with the born-agains then the Jehovah's Witnesses.

Kieran and Esther became very taken with Teddy, and he felt like a second son to them by the time the visit came to an end. Kieran made

Rhonda promise that they would stop by again on the way back to DC. He had never met someone in his twenties who knew so much about politics, religion, and the world. Rhonda's past dates had been so clueless that this deaf man was like a rush of fresh air in a stale room. He had been so wrong to label Teddy a "mute" and use derogatory language to describe him before even shaking his hand. He vowed to tell Rhonda soon that Teddy had his blessing for future purposes. She would be happy to hear that.

Finally, Thursday morning arrived and they went outside to Rhonda's car. Everyone hugged each other. Kieran and Esther looked forward to seeing Teddy again and their daughter had never looked so radiant as she did now. They were thrilled to have such a nice young man. At this point, his deafness was just a footnote for them. They learned more phrases and they had promised to keep learning. They were going to look for ASL classes in the area and if they could not find anything, they would hire a tutor so by the time they saw Teddy again, they could communicate on a basic level.

Rhonda pulled the car out of the driveway, then waved at her folks. She was so proud of them and the way they had conducted themselves during the two-day visit. She could see that Mom and Dad had been really entertained by Teddy's great sense of humor and storytelling. She had never met a man like him, except for Dad, and she considered herself very lucky because women who saw Teddy assumed he was a nerd and bookworm who was boring.

She had found out otherwise, solely by accident. He had made a comment when they met each other for the second time. She couldn't remember right now what he had said, but it was at the campus security office. It had something to do with the campus police being "wannabes" and she had laughed. That was the first clue of many.

Why so many women were fixated on chiseled physiques, abs, and rugged jawlines, she could never guess. Their loss, her gain! What was ironic about their conversation was that even though these campus cops (he had referred to them as the Keystone Kops, or KK for short) worked at the only liberal arts university in the world for deaf students, they signed at a very rudimentary level.

Their conversation was too fast for them to catch so they felt safe in mocking these KKs who were supposed to be fluent signers because they worked on a campus with over 1,000 deaf undergraduates. It was a running joke among students that they needed a hearing interpreter anytime a KK came over to them and asked questions. Teddy had been frustrated when he tried to communicate with one of the officers and she came to his assistance. Later, they had walked back to the dorms after she finished her business of getting a student ID card. In a way, they owed their relationship to these KKs, so it was a silver lining in the clouds.

It was a short ten-minute ride to Teddy's hometown. He was apprehensive about her meeting his parents because of their staunch support of audism and never learning ASL. Teddy also was coming from an experience where he had met a set of parents very motivated to become fluent in ASL for his welfare. All of the conversations the four of them had while eating out had been so much fun and full of laughter. There was no way his parents could top that at all.

Before they knew it, the sign for Exit 33 – Lakeville Road came into view. They got off the Long Island Expressway and went north onto Lakeville Road. It was approximately two minutes north of the expressway when they got to the street where his parents lived. Teddy motioned for her to turn right at the traffic light, then a left at the first corner. The house was right there near the railroad tracks. It was a family joke that nobody could sleep with the house standing so close to the tracks except for Teddy. Everyone else wore earplugs when they went to sleep. It was a must-have accessory for them.

Rhonda wondered what it would be like to sleep in such proximity to the tracks. There was only one way to find out. She had earplugs from when she attended deaf culture class on campus so that would be an experience for her to go through. Of course, they would sleep separately just like they had at her folks' house. It was hard, but the proper thing to do out of respect for the "older generation."

The Fitzgerald homestead was really nice, with a huge front lawn. There was an oak tree blocking the view of the front door. It was just starting to bloom, with spring coming. Two cars lined the driveway, so she pulled into the side to keep it open for his folks' cars. He had told her that was the best thing to do. She turned the engine off and they sat there looking at each other. This was going to be tougher, and they knew it. Their hands clasped and Teddy moved in to kiss her on the cheeks, just to show her how much he appreciated having her with him on this visit home.

The front door opened and she saw his parents come out. She was surprised to see how young they looked. As Teddy was twenty-four, she knew they were forty-seven years old. When Teddy was born, they had both been twenty-three years of age. That was very common back then in the fifties, unlike today, as many couples now waited longer before getting married. People were maturing later in life and did not feel as ready at such a young age to get hitched to someone.

Teddy cleared his throat and he took Rhonda's hand, walking toward his parents, who were walking down the driveway already. This was it. He hugged them and looked at Rhonda.

"Mom, Dad – this is my girlfriend, Rhonda." It felt really good to call her his girlfriend. He had never had one before. In fact, his dating prospects in school had been so dismal that at his eighth grade prom, he asked ten girls to dance with him, all of them rejecting the proposal based on their irrational fear of his deafness at the time, even the last one, who had a serious physical ailment from when she had been unable to breathe at birth except through a tube in the trachea. When she walked away quickly from him toward her father who had just arrived, Teddy knew he was done probably for the next four years until graduation. His prediction came true.

"Hello, Rhonda! Welcome to our home. You can call us Jack and Elise. We are thrilled that our son has brought home a girlfriend, especially someone as pretty as you!"

Teddy's dad was really nice, Rhonda thought with a bemused expression. She had her walls up because of Teddy's many stories about their slowness to accept his deafness. Even now, she could see them staring at Teddy's ears to check and see if he was wearing any hearing aids. Was that the most important thing to check for after not seeing their son for months, especially after such a momentous week on the Gallaudet campus?

"Son…" Jack paused, his eyes fixated on Teddy's face. "You are not wearing any hearing aids. How come? You spent a lot of money on a hearing aid and mold a few years ago and we would like you to be able to hear us calling your name."

Teddy seethed. Already they were making a scene, in front of his girlfriend? His mind raced back many years to the numerous taunts he had endured from neighboring kids about the devices that rested behind his ears. They were visible even though he let his hair grow a little longer. Many times, the aids emitted feedback because the molds were loose or did not fit right. What right did they have to lecture him about wearing these aids, even though he was an independent young adult who lived away from home?

"Look, I decided not to wear any aids for a good reason. Rhonda has never mentioned it and doesn't make a big deal out of it. If she wants my attention, she simply taps me on the shoulder or hand. Or if she is far away, she flicks the light switch. Simple!"

He felt funny talking to them without signing in front of Rhonda. What a change from being with her parents just that morning and over the past two days. He had felt carefree and relaxed.

Now, he was all tensed up, feeling the same pressure he always felt when he came to see them. Yes, he loved them because they were his parents. They had worked hard to make sure he had a good education and excellent speech and lipreading skills. But…a big but…he had paid a huge price for it with his extremely weak social skills and stunted emotional judgment, which had manifested itself many times.

On purpose, he had left their bags in the car. Rhonda had started to grab them, but he told her not to bother just yet. If things continued in this fashion, they could always turn around and go back to her parents' house. The incident with his parents in Florida just this past Christmas still burned in his mind. Nobody had ever apologized to him for anything that had happened over the past twenty-four years. They sure as heck were not going to start that anytime soon.

Rhonda stood back watching this exchange between her boyfriend and his father. Poor Teddy! She already could see what he was talking about with their denial of his deafness. She saw that Elise, his mom, stood quietly by as the two men sparred verbally.

"Dad, you keep telling me that wearing hearing aids is like having eyeglasses to help one see. But those are two completely different things. Someone can function without hearing aids, while eyeglasses are a much more crucial part of somebody's everyday routine. Why do you and Mom keep harping on about this? Are you going to keep doing that as long as we are here?"

The tension in the air was so thick that even though they were outside and there was a cool breeze, they could feel in the air. It felt very awkward. Teddy was so tempted to leave right there and then, sparing Rhonda from having to suffer through his humiliation that he had experienced time and time again. Yet he vowed to stick it out just one day so she could see first-hand what he had been talking about all this time with his parents and two sisters.

The front door opened again. Teddy's middle sister, Rosemary, came out with Kathleen right behind her. He introduced them to Rhonda and everyone started chattering away. This was nothing new for him. He took Rhonda's hand and they walked toward the front door to go inside the house, leaving his family behind. He wanted to get away from a familiar experience of being left out. He refused to have Rhonda interpret for him like she had at her parents' because it was important for her to see what he lived through here in his hometown.

Once they were inside, Rhonda was struck by the simplicity of the house's interior. In front of her was a cozy family room with a sofa at the far wall. There were countless portraits of the three children and the parents in different settings on the wall. She laughed at the ones with the kids on Santa's lap. She saw a charcoal drawing of ice skates on the wall. Who had done such a masterpiece? She walked over to check the artist's signature. It couldn't be! Teddy in 1978? He was only fourteen years old at the time. Wow! She would have to ask him about that another time. He hadn't told her about his artistic talents.

The rest of the house was really full of memorabilia. There was a door ajar that presumably led to a closet. She could see marks on the far left above the knob. Puzzled, she walked over and saw names and dates with the height of each mark. She turned around and asked Teddy about it. He explained that it was a family tradition to mark how tall each kid was every now and then. His growth spurt had ended and now it was his sisters' turn to mark theirs. She thought it was very cute, but it had nothing to do with his struggles growing up in this house.

She could only imagine how many memories Teddy had in each room. There was the family room where he had spent many frustrating moments watching TV and not being able to find out what was being said before the advent of the caption decoder in 1980. There was the small dining table in the kitchen where he had spent many holidays sitting at a family dinner for special occasions. She could feel the specter of disappointment and loneliness emanating from there. She was so sensitive, having heard many of his stories from when he grew up there.

She felt overwhelmed at seeing everything in the house, because she had heard stories from him over the weeks and months prior to coming here. He had been very explicit about what the rooms looked like and what had happened in each one. Later, she saw the bedroom where Teddy used to sleep. There was a whole wall full of books. Many were from his father's time, business books that did nothing but collect dust. Some of the books were Teddy's from high school, including the von Daniken book that was his all-time favorite. She vowed to buy him a brand-new copy for his next birthday.

She knew he had been an avid reader partly to escape the loneliness and ostracization of his childhood. When he was reading a book, there was no feeling that he missed anything around him. He could use his imagination and picture a movie happening in his mind. His vocabulary, as a result, was far superior to any other student at Gallaudet that he had met over the last few months. His command of English idioms and syntax was not the commonly found level that most deaf people had. It was no wonder that he had been offered a huge scholarship when he applied to Gallaudet during his senior year of high school.

Looking at the wide range of book titles, she laughed when she saw the *MAD* magazines. Teddy was standing beside her and he commented that these issues had really kept him abreast of the popular media at the time. His favorite issue was the one lampooning the then-popular movie *Jaws*. He had not seen that with captions or any other movie out in the theater except for *The Silent Movie* with Mel Brooks. She had heard about his experience laughing in the theater, louder than anyone else. His sisters had shushed him repeatedly, as they were embarrassed by the loudness of his voice when he laughed.

As she passed the bathroom upstairs, another hilarious story popped into her head that Teddy had told her recently before DPN. At Thanksgiving one year, he and his family had gathered upstate at Uncle Benny's house in Carmel for a special meal. His maternal grandparents had been alive then. What happened was that he got stuck in the bathroom and because he was deaf, there was no way to communicate through the door! They had to resort to writing on sheets of paper and sliding them under the door. His dad had to walk around the house and get into the bathroom from an outside window. After struggling for an hour, they finally got the bathroom door open!

Dinner was awkward at best, as his parents and sisters talked incessantly about inane topics. Rhonda could hear and understand most of what was being said, but she sat there quietly watching Teddy eat without contributing a single word to the conversation taking place right in front of him. She could see the pain that was evident in his eyes.

He ate very quickly, cleaning off his plate. He pushed his chair away and looked at all of them without saying a word. His head jerked to his right, beckoning her to leave the table with him, as she was not eating much. She had lost her appetite witnessing this entire situation as it unfolded in front of her. So, it was fine with her that they left the table before everyone else was finished.

Elise stopped talking in mid-sentence and her head turned in Teddy's direction. She did not look very pleased, and she put her silverware down. She wiped the edges of her mouth with a napkin and sighed.

"Teddy, where are you going? You know the family rule is steadfast: no leaving the table until everyone is finished!" The nerve of her son, getting up in the middle of a family discussion. When would he ever learn to respect his parents and sisters? Didn't he realize how lucky he was to have grown up in a nice house like this with a stay-at-home mom and a successful dad? He had never wanted for anything, and yet he was being so rude in front of his new girlfriend! The sheer audacity.

"Mom, you know why I am leaving the table. It is the same as always, never changed since I was living here as a kid. I have always left the table when I am done eating." In fact, he had started doing it in the last two years of high school, but he didn't want to belabor that point. He was not going to stand for it anymore. His girlfriend did not deserve to feel uncomfortable here.

All of a sudden, Jack got up, and his face was contorted with rage. His hands grabbed Teddy by the shoulders and as he talked, his whole body shook. Teddy looked ashen in the face, but he didn't say anything.

"You are going to sit down. Period. Both of you! Or leave this house!"

That was easy, thought Teddy, with a sudden sense of calmness. His father had given him a way out. Just a second ago, he had been totally unsure what to do in this situation. Now he knew. His whole existence of fighting long against sorrow was over. He was ready to move on with his new life as a proud deaf person who had been transformed as a result of DPN. Never again would he accept being oppressed, ignored, or shunned by anyone. Even if that meant being kicked out of his own family.

Gathering his wits, he calmly peeled off his father's clutching hands finger by finger. Then, he turned toward Rhonda and signed, "Let's go. Our bags are in the car. We do not need to stand for this any longer. They have no idea what I am saying." He could see that Rhonda had a very surprised look on her face; then she recovered quickly, understanding the magnitude of this very moment. It was just like that millisecond when he had stepped off the curb onto the street that fateful Sunday night, March 6th, 1988. This was going to be a watershed moment in her boyfriend's life.

Before anyone could react, Teddy and Rhonda stepped out of the house, walking quickly to her car. They got in, Rhonda driving. She didn't want him to be at the wheel after going through an emotional incident like this. She wanted him to calm down and get himself back together. They knew they were going back to her parents' house, a place of safety for both. It had been a cocoon for the past few days. They couldn't wait to get back there.

She could hear the yelling as they pulled out of the driveway and drove down the street toward the expressway. She would not tell Teddy because it would only serve to exacerbate his confusion and disturbed mental state at the moment. Maybe later she would tell him, but not yet. As they barreled down the street, Teddy's breathing eventually slowed and his hands stopped shaking. He began to sob and his chest heaved repeatedly. She had a box of Kleenex in the back seat, so she reached back with her right hand and took a tissue to give to him.

They didn't dare stop the car, because one of his parents could catch up to him. Luckily, they didn't know where Rhonda lived, nor her last name, so they would be unable to locate her parents' home. She let him be and just kept driving. She knew where she was and how to get back to Mom and Dad. That was her primary objective right now. When they got there, the three of them would take good care of him and he would be fine.

It had been surreal for her to witness the entire scene. Could she imagine going through that day in, day out, for years and years? No! The emotional and mental toll on Teddy had to be monumental. She knew he would be OK, but it would not happen overnight. She would take care of her new man and it remained to be seen whether his parents would ever come around to support their only son. It was really sad that they had never tailored their lives around a deaf person. But Teddy Fitzgerald was a very good person and his long fight against sorrow would come to an end with her immersion in ASL. Also, her best friend and ex-roommate Syd was becoming involved with Howie. So she could see many happy times ahead of them.

CPSIA information can be obtained at www.ICGtesting.com
Printed in the USA
BVOW031930040413

317335BV00002B/263/P